SERIOUSLY
GOOD SALADS

SERIOUSLY GOOD SALADS

Creative Flavor Combinations for
Nutritious, Satisfying Meals

**NICKY
CORBISHLEY**

Founder of
Kitchen Sanctuary

PAGE STREET
PUBLISHING CO.

PAGE STREET
PUBLISHING CO.

First published in 2019 by
Page Street Publishing Co.
27 Congress Street, Suite 105
Salem, MA 01970
www.pagestreetpublishing.com

Distributed by Macmillan, sales in Canada by The Canadian Manda Group.

23   22   21   20   19   1   2   3   4   5

ISBN-13: 978-1-62414-825-5
ISBN-10: 1-62414-825-5

Library of Congress Control Number: 2018962644

Cover and book design by Kylie Alexander for Page Street Publishing Co.
Photography by Nicky Corbishley

Printed and bound in China

To Chris, Gracey and Lewis,
Thank you for always cheering me on
(and for eating salad for two months straight!) xx

CONTENTS

INTRODUCTION

I've always loved experimenting with food.

Working all day in a corporate job, I used to come home and head straight into the kitchen to unwind. My kitchen is my sanctuary, so it seemed fitting that when I left my job to try something new, I would put all my effort into my food blog, Kitchen Sanctuary.

Since that day almost five years ago, my love for food and cooking has only increased. My husband, Chris, left his job, too, and now Kitchen Sanctuary is our family business.

We spend our days creating recipes, photographing and filming them and, of course, eating.

Lots of eating.

All that eating means that balance is important to us. Yes, I'm going to eat *all* the naughty stuff (it's not unheard-of for me to be making chocolate cake at eleven o'clock at night because I'm watching a movie with my husband and I forgot to buy the necessary gluttonous snacks, and I *need* treats), but I balance it out with nutritious, good-for-you foods, too.

Life is boring when you just stick to one side. I haven't got the willpower to live off salad leaves and quinoa. Even a menu of pizza, fries and chocolate cake, although fun for a day, soon gets boring.

If I balance it out, I enjoy both, and that's the purpose of this book.

Eating what you love.

Food that's delicious and satisfying, with elements that might be considered a little naughty (my buttermilk chicken might be deep-fried, but it's good for the soul), balanced out with vibrant, nutritious and, above all, tasty ingredients.

Layer those flavors, drizzle with those dressings and include different textures and a rainbow of colors.

It's not about taking your burger and fries and serving it with a wilted little salad that you'll probably push to one side anyway. It's about incorporating those good-for-you elements as a major player in the meal. Flavors that work together.

I want to smash the preconception that salads are just "diet food."

Seriously Good Salads is full of salads that make you want to eat. Every. Single. Bite.

Nickey

TIPS AND TRICKS

Here are a few little tips and tricks I've learned over the years to get the most out of your salads.

- Go for lots of different textures. Nobody wants to chew through a salad made up purely of leaves. A variety of textures (and flavors) makes for a much more satisfying salad.

- Don't be afraid to add fruit to your salads—sliced nectarines, grapes, apples and pears are a great addition, but you can also add citrus fruits, berries and dried fruits.

- Serve tomatoes at room temperature—dark red tomatoes, still on the vine, are the sweetest, most flavorful kind.

- A simple salad dressing makes a huge difference to any salad. Make up a larger batch of your favorite dressing, then keep it in the refrigerator to use during the week.

- Add salad dressings right before serving to prevent the leaves from wilting.

- Brush cut avocados, apples and pears with lemon juice to prevent their browning too quickly.

- Make it portable—place firmer, heavier salad ingredients, such as tomatoes and eggs, on the bottom of your bowl, and lighter, more delicate ingredients, such as leaves and herbs, on the top. Store the dressing separately.

- If making a mason jar salad, the same rules apply, but you can place the salad dressing at the bottom of the jar, then top the dressing with ingredients that are less likely to absorb it—such as whole grape tomatoes—before layering on the rest of the ingredients. You'll need to keep the jar upright to prevent the dressing from mixing with the rest of the ingredients before you eat. Tip out onto a plate or bowl to eat.

MIGHTY MEAT AND POULTRY

For me, the easiest way to make a salad feel like a full and satisfying meal is by including meat.

Chicken is an easy favorite that works with most cuisines (you'll find 10-plus chicken recipes in this book), but I'm also including recipes with steak, such as my juicy Coffee-Crusted Seared Steak Bowl (page 35) and my spicy Bulgogi Beef Lettuce Wraps (page 41), pork (you haven't lived till you've tried my Sticky Pork Belly [page 58]) and even duck (Chinese-style with *perfectly* crispy skin in my Chinese Duck Salad with Plums [page 69]).

- Use leftover meat—such as leftover cooked chicken in my Crispy Chicken Shredded Salad with Honey Mustard Dressing (page 23).

- Use ready-cooked, prepared or cured meat, such as the selection of meats on my Piled-High Cured Meat Deli Board (page 46).

- Take your time and cook from scratch—how about my Firecracker Chicken and Wild Rice Nourish Bowl (page 14), made with chicken marinated in my special spicy marinade, then grilled to perfectly charred deliciousness?

If you're not a meat lover, the other 40-plus meat-free and fish-based salads have got you covered.

FIRECRACKER CHICKEN AND WILD RICE NOURISH BOWL

This spicy chicken salad with a sweet-and-sour sriracha dressing is easily filling enough for dinner and it makes a great winter salad for a cold evening. It takes a little bit of time to prepare and marinate, but it's so worth the wait!

SERVES 4

To marinate the chicken, in a large bowl, stir together all the marinade ingredients except the chicken and oil. Add the chicken, then cover and refrigerate for at least an hour or overnight.

Brush a cast-iron grill pan or skillet with the oil and heat over high heat until hot. Scoop the chicken out of the marinade with a slotted spoon, place on the pan and cook, turning once, until browned and cooked through, 5 to 6 minutes total. Discard the marinade.

In a small pitcher, stir together all the dressing ingredients.

(continued)

MARINADE AND CHICKEN

½ tsp red pepper flakes

1 tbsp (15 ml) sriracha

2 cloves garlic, peeled and minced

3 tbsp (38 g) light brown sugar

2 tbsp (30 ml) light soy sauce

1 tbsp (15 ml) dark soy sauce

1 tbsp (16 g) tomato paste

1½ tsp (8 ml) cider vinegar

1½ tsp (8 g) tamarind paste

1½ tsp (8 ml) Asian fish sauce

Pinch of ground white pepper

3 medium chicken breasts, sliced into bite-size chunks

1 tbsp (15 ml) vegetable oil

SRIRACHA DRESSING

2 tbsp (30 ml) olive oil

1 tbsp (15 ml) sriracha

1 small clove garlic, peeled and minced

1½ tbsp (30 g) honey

Juice of ½ lime

Pinch of salt

Pinch of freshly ground black pepper

Divide the baby salad leaves among 4 serving bowls. Arrange the cooked rice, avocado, red cabbage, radishes, red and yellow bell peppers, snap peas and grape tomatoes in the bowls.

Push 2 of the pieces of toasted flatbread into the edge of each bowl, then spoon one-quarter of the cooked chicken on top of each salad.

Sprinkle with the scallions, shichimi and black and white sesame seeds, then garnish each bowl with a lime wedge before serving. Serve with the dressing.

NOTE: *Shichimi togarashi* is a Japanese spice mixture containing 7 spices. There are variations, but most contain black pepper, chiles, citrus zest, sesame seeds, ginger, dried seaweed and poppy seeds. You can buy it online or from Asian supermarkets.

SALAD

2 cups (60 g) packed baby salad leaves

1½ cups (250 g) cooked wild red rice (from about ½ cup [99 g] raw), warm or cold

1 ripe avocado, peeled, pitted and sliced

¼ red cabbage, finely sliced (about 11 oz [312 g] sliced)

2 radishes, thinly sliced

1 red bell pepper, seeded and thinly sliced

1 yellow bell pepper, seeded and thinly sliced

1 cup (85 g) snap peas

10 grape tomatoes, sliced in half

2 flatbreads, toasted or grilled and quartered

2 scallions, sliced into thin strips

1 tsp shichimi togarashi (see Note)

1 tsp black sesame seeds

1 tsp white sesame seeds

4 lime wedges

PORTUGUESE CHICKEN SALAD WITH GRILLED BELL PEPPERS

The homemade piri piri sauce in this recipe is used as a marinade for the chicken and bell peppers, and also makes up part of the simple creamy dressing.

The sauce is so delicious—packed with layers of flavors and a nice kick of heat. I like to double the amount when I make it, so I have some left in the refrigerator for the week.

SERVES 4

First, prepare the piri piri sauce. In a large saucepan, heat the olive oil over medium heat, then add the onion. Cook, stirring often, for 5 minutes, or until softened.

Add the garlic, bell pepper and chiles and cook for an additional 3 minutes, stirring often. Add the tomatoes, paprika, oregano, salt, pepper, lime juice, vinegar and brown sugar, and cook for an additional 2 minutes, stirring often. Turn off the heat and let cool. Once cool, blend with an immersion blender until almost smooth (it's nice to have a little bit of texture in there).

Next, prepare the dressing. In a bowl, stir together ¼ cup (60 ml) of the piri piri sauce with the mayonnaise and cilantro. Cover and place in the refrigerator.

(continued)

PIRI PIRI SAUCE

1½ tsp (8 ml) olive oil

I large onion, diced

3 cloves garlic, peeled and roughly chopped

I red bell pepper, seeded and chopped

6 to 12 bird's eye chiles, roughly chopped (depending on how hot you like it)

2 vine-ripened tomatoes, quartered

I tsp paprika

I tsp dried oregano

I tsp salt

½ tsp freshly ground black pepper

Juice of ½ lime

2 tbsp (30 ml) red wine vinegar

2 tbsp (27 g) light brown sugar

CREAMY PIRI PIRI DRESSING

¼ cup (60 g) mayonnaise

⅓ cup (10 g) finely chopped fresh cilantro

Prepare the chicken and peppers: In a bowl, combine all but 2 tablespoons (30 ml) of the remaining piri piri sauce, the chicken and the olive oil. Stir to coat, then cover and refrigerate for 1 hour.

Heat a cast-iron grill pan until very hot, remove the chicken from the refrigerator and place the breasts in a single layer on the pan. They should start to sizzle. Let the chicken cook for a couple of minutes, until browned, then use tongs to turn it over. Continue to cook until the chicken is cooked all the way through. You can test this by slicing the chicken at the thickest part and ensuring it's hot and no longer pink in the middle.

Transfer the chicken to a cutting board to rest for 5 minutes, then slice.

Meanwhile, brush the remaining 2 tablespoons (30 ml) of piri piri sauce on the bell pepper slices, then place on the grill pan and cook for 3 to 4 minutes, or until lightly charred. Remove from the pan.

Arrange one-quarter of the baby salad leaves, cucumber, tomatoes and potatoes in each of 4 bowls.

Top with the chicken and peppers, then arrange the onion rings on top. Drizzle with the creamy piri piri dressing and serve topped with the cilantro.

CHICKEN AND PEPPERS

3 chicken breasts, flattened using a rolling pin

1½ tbsp (23 ml) olive oil

1 red bell pepper, seeded and sliced

1 green bell pepper, seeded and sliced

1 yellow bell pepper, seeded and sliced

SALAD

3 cups (90 g) packed baby salad leaves

1 cucumber, peeled, seeded and sliced

4 vine-ripened tomatoes, quartered

8 cooked baby new potatoes, skin on, sliced

½ small red onion, sliced into thin rings

½ small yellow onion, sliced into thin rings

⅓ cup (10 g) chopped fresh cilantro

CHIPOTLE CHICKEN COBB SALAD

A bit of a twist on the original Cobb salad, I'm forgoing the cheese and eggs and making a spicier version with chipotle chicken and homemade tortilla strips. You can also replace the chicken with halloumi to make a delicious vegetarian version.

SERVES 4

In a large bowl, stir together all the marinade ingredients except the chicken, add the chicken and mix to coat. Cover and refrigerate for at least an hour or overnight.

When ready to cook, prepare the tortilla strips by first preheating the oven to 400°F (204°C).

Slice the tortillas into ½-inch (1.3-cm) strips and place on a large baking sheet. Drizzle with the oil, then sprinkle with the paprika, cumin, salt and pepper. Use your hands to toss everything together and then spread it all out into one layer. Toast in the oven for 5 to 6 minutes, or until the tortilla strips are golden brown (keep an eye on them after 3 minutes to ensure they don't burn). Remove from the oven and transfer to a plate. Set aside until ready to serve.

Heat a cast-iron grill pan over medium to high heat and brush it with oil. When hot, place the ear of corn on the pan and cook, turning regularly, for 7 to 10 minutes, or until lightly charred. Transfer to a cutting board and carefully slice off the corn kernels.

Remove the chicken from the refrigerator and place on the grill pan, discarding the marinade. Cook for 4 to 5 minutes on each side, or until browned and cooked all the way through. You can test this by slicing the chicken at the thickest part and ensuring it's hot and no longer pink in the middle.

Place the chicken on a cutting board and roughly chop.

In a small bowl, stir together all the vinaigrette ingredients.

On a large salad platter, arrange the lettuce, avocado, tomatoes, black beans, chicken, corn and tortilla strips in rows.

Serve with the cilantro lime vinaigrette.

CHIPOTLE MARINADE AND CHICKEN

2 tbsp (30 ml) vegetable oil

1 tsp chipotle chile powder

1 tsp smoked paprika

½ tsp salt

½ tsp dried oregano

½ tsp ground cumin

½ tsp garlic salt

½ tsp freshly ground black pepper

3 chicken breasts, flattened

HOMEMADE TORTILLA STRIPS

2 whole wheat tortillas

2 tbsp (30 ml) olive oil

½ tsp paprika

¼ tsp ground cumin

¼ tsp salt

Pinch of freshly ground black pepper

SALAD

Oil, for pan

1 ear of corn

2 heads romaine lettuce, shredded

1 avocado, peeled, pitted and chopped into small chunks

12 grape tomatoes, sliced in half

1 (15-oz [425-g]) can black beans, drained and rinsed

CILANTRO LIME VINAIGRETTE

2 tbsp (30 ml) fresh lime juice

1 tsp white wine vinegar

½ clove garlic, minced

1 tbsp (20 g) honey

Pinch of salt and pepper

3 tbsp (45 ml) extra virgin olive oil

2 tbsp (5 g) finely chopped fresh cilantro

CRISPY CHICKEN SHREDDED SALAD WITH HONEY MUSTARD DRESSING

This recipe uses leftover cooked chicken that's shredded and seasoned before being lightly fried to perfect crispiness. Served on top of piles of crunchy salad, it's utterly satisfying.

You can also use leftover cooked beef, pork or lamb, which makes it a great salad after a roast dinner.

I like to use a mandoline to slice the veggies in super-quick time. It also helps to ensure the slices are uniform, which I think looks prettier in the bowl.

SERVES 4

In a large skillet, heat the oil over high heat.

Meanwhile, sprinkle the shredded chicken with the cornstarch, salt, garlic salt, pepper and paprika and toss together to evenly coat.

Fry the shredded chicken in the oil until golden brown and crispy, for 4 to 5 minutes. You may need to do this in 2 batches. Remove the fried chicken from the oil and transfer to a bowl lined with paper towels to remove any excess oil. If cooking in batches, keep the first batch warm in a 150 to 200°F (65 to 90°C) oven while you fry the rest.

In a small bowl, stir together all the dressing ingredients.

In a large serving bowl, arrange the lettuce, cabbage, carrots, cucumber, bell pepper, apple and radishes.

Top with the crispy chicken, scallions and smoked almonds.

Serve with the honey mustard dressing.

CRISPY CHICKEN

¼ cup (60 ml) vegetable oil

2 cooked chicken breasts, roughly shredded

3 tbsp (24 g) cornstarch

¼ tsp salt

¼ tsp garlic salt

¼ tsp freshly ground black pepper

½ tsp paprika

HONEY MUSTARD DRESSING

¼ cup (60 ml) olive oil

2 tsp (10 ml) white wine vinegar

3 tbsp (60 g) honey

2 tsp (8 g) Dijon mustard

Pinch of salt

Pinch of freshly ground black pepper

SHREDDED SALAD

2 heads romaine lettuce, shredded

¼ red cabbage, sliced into thin strips, using a mandoline (about 11 oz [312 g] sliced)

2 carrots, peeled and sliced into thin strips, using a mandoline

1 cucumber, sliced into thin strips, using a mandoline

1 red bell pepper, sliced into thin strips, using a mandoline

1 sweet eating apple, sliced into thin strips, using a mandoline (mix with 1 tsp of fresh lemon juice to prevent browning after slicing)

3 radishes, quartered

4 scallions, sliced into thin strips

¼ cup (24 g) smoked almonds, roughly chopped

STICKY CHICKEN SALAD

This recipe is based on one of my favorite stir-fries. Only, for this salad, I'm leaving the vegetables raw!

More crunch, less cooking time, no risk of overcooking those veggies and ending up with one of those stir-fries where everything is a bit brown and boring looking. You can serve the chicken hot or cold—so, it makes a great packed lunch.

SERVES 4

Place the chicken in a bowl. In a separate bowl, stir together the soy sauce, honey, sweet chili sauce, garlic, ginger, sesame oil, mirin, rice vinegar and sherry. Pour half of this mixture over the chicken. Cover and chill in the refrigerator for an hour or two.

Whisk 2 tablespoons (30 ml) of the olive oil into the remaining soy sauce mixture, cover and set aside. This will become the dressing for the salad.

In a large skillet, heat the remaining tablespoon (15 ml) of olive oil over medium-high heat. Add the chicken and fry, stirring often, until the chicken is browned on the outside and no longer pink in the middle, 5 to 6 minutes total. Turn off the heat.

Divide the noodles, baby kale, red and yellow bell peppers, carrot, cucumber and scallions among 4 bowls.

Top with the cooked chicken and sprinkle with the chopped chile and sesame seeds. Serve with a drizzle of the reserved dressing.

TIP: To make this a stir-fry version, add all the salad ingredients (I'd replace the cucumber with zucchini), except the sesame seeds, to the pan of cooked chicken and add the reserved dressing. Fry for 2 to 3 minutes, then sprinkle with the sesame seeds to serve.

CHICKEN AND MARINADE

1 lb (454 g) chicken breast, chopped into bite-size chunks

¼ cup (60 ml) dark soy sauce

2 tbsp (40 g) honey

1 tbsp (20 g) sweet chili sauce

2 cloves garlic, peeled and minced

1 tsp minced fresh ginger

1½ tbsp (23 ml) sesame oil

½ tsp mirin

½ tsp rice vinegar

1 tbsp (15 ml) dry sherry

3 tbsp (45 ml) olive oil, divided

SALAD

2 cups (320 g) cooked medium egg noodles, cold

2 cups (60 g) baby kale

1 red bell pepper, seeded and sliced

1 yellow bell pepper, seeded and sliced

1 large carrot, spiralized or sliced into thin strips

1 cucumber, spiralized or sliced into thin strips

4 scallions, sliced

1 red chile pepper, sliced into thin strips

1 tsp mixed black and white sesame seeds

MEXICAN GRILLED CHICKEN AND CORN SALAD WITH SOUR CREAM DRESSING

A spicy, filling salad with a cool creamy dressing. I love serving this with blue corn nacho chips, for an extra treat.

Flattening the chicken breasts before cooking helps tenderize the meat, and also means it cooks quicker and more evenly. I tend to place my chicken in a large freezer bag before bashing with a rolling pin. It's rather satisfying after a stressful day!

SERVES 4

In a bowl, combine all the chicken ingredients. Mix together, cover and refrigerate for 1 to 2 hours.

Heat a cast-iron grill pan over medium-high heat and brush with oil. Add the chicken and cook for 4 to 5 minutes on each side, or until browned and cooked all the way through. You can test this by slicing the chicken at the thickest part and ensuring it's hot and no longer pink in the middle.

Turn off the heat and transfer to a cutting board. Let cool for a few minutes, then slice into strips.

In a small bowl, stir together all the dressing ingredients.

In a large serving bowl, arrange the corn, tomatoes, avocado, lettuce, cilantro, red onion and eggs.

Add the nacho chips, pushing them into one side of the bowl.

Top the salad with the cooked chicken and drizzle with the dressing before serving. Serve with blue corn nacho chips.

MEXICAN CHICKEN

3 chicken breasts, flattened using a rolling pin

2 tbsp (30 ml) vegetable oil, plus more for pan

½ tsp salt

½ tsp freshly ground black pepper

Juice of 1 lime

1 tbsp (20 g) honey

2 tbsp (15 g) fajita spice

1 large clove garlic, peeled and minced

3 tbsp (8 g) finely chopped fresh cilantro

SOUR CREAM DRESSING

¼ cup (60 g) sour cream

2 tbsp (28 g) mayonnaise

1 tsp Dijon mustard

1 tsp fresh lime juice

½ tsp garlic powder

¼ tsp salt

Pinch of ground white pepper

3 tbsp (45 ml) water

CORN SALAD

1 cup (175 g) cooked fresh or canned corn

10 mixed red and yellow grape tomatoes, sliced in half

1 avocado, peeled, pitted and sliced

1 head romaine lettuce, roughly chopped

3 tbsp (8 g) chopped fresh cilantro

½ red onion, sliced

2 hard-boiled large eggs, quartered

1½ oz (43 g) blue corn nacho chips

CHICKEN CAESAR PASTA SALAD WITH ROASTED VEGETABLES

This is a hearty and filling salad, which makes it perfect for dinner all year round. I'm using red onion and zucchini, but you can use whatever vegetables are in season—broccoli, tomatoes, squash, bell peppers—all make great swaps.

Serve this salad with my Easy Caesar Dressing, for minimal fuss. This is a simpler and quicker version than a classic Caesar dressing, which uses raw egg yolk and requires lots of whisking.

SERVES 4

Preheat the oven to 400°F (204°C).

Place the red onion wedges and chicken breasts on a baking sheet. Drizzle with 2 tablespoons (30 ml) of the oil and half of the salt and pepper. Toss to coat and then bake for 10 minutes.

Add the zucchini cubes to the pan and turn them over to coat with the oil. Return the pan to the oven and bake for an additional 10 minutes.

Meanwhile, place the cubed ciabatta on a separate baking sheet and drizzle with the remaining tablespoon (15 ml) of oil. Sprinkle with the remaining salt and pepper, and toast in the oven for 5 to 7 minutes, until the ciabatta has browned and the chicken on the other pan is cooked through. Remove from the oven.

In a small bowl, whisk together all the dressing ingredients.

Arrange the lettuce on a large serving plate.

Slice the chicken into bite-size chunks and place on top of the lettuce along with the cooked pasta, roasted vegetables and ciabatta croutons.

Drizzle with a little of the dressing and top with the shredded Parmesan.

Serve with extra dressing.

2 red onions, cut into wedges

2 chicken breasts

3 tbsp (45 ml) olive oil, divided

½ tsp salt

½ tsp freshly ground black pepper

1 medium zucchini, chopped into 1" (2.5-cm) cubes

1 ciabatta bread, chopped into 1" (2.5-cm) cubes

2 heads romaine lettuce, leaves separated and washed

2 cups (300 g) cooked and cooled spiral pasta

2 tbsp (10 g) shredded Parmesan cheese

EASY CAESAR DRESSING

2 anchovies, mashed with a fork

1 clove garlic, peeled and minced

Juice of ½ lemon

1 tsp Dijon mustard

5 tbsp (70 g) mayonnaise

1 tbsp (15 ml) white wine vinegar

3 tbsp (15 g) shredded Parmesan cheese

GREEK SALAD WITH HUMMUS AND SHREDDED SOUVLAKI CHICKEN

Over the years, I've visited quite a few Greek islands, and it's fair to say I probably eat my own weight in souvlaki and Greek salad every time I go. I do have to come clean, though. I'm not keen on kalamata olives—which are often served with Greek salad. I've been trying to train myself to love olives for years, but so far I've only managed to enjoy one variety—the Nocellara olive, which is actually from Sicily. I call it my training olive.

SERVES 4

In a bowl, combine all the chicken ingredients. Stir together and cover, then refrigerate for an hour or two.

Divide all the salad ingredients, except the hummus, among 4 plates or arrange on a single large platter.

In a small bowl, whisk together all the dressing ingredients.

Pour half of the dressing over the salad and toss together. Spoon the hummus onto the salad.

Heat a cast-iron grill pan until very hot, then place the chicken in a single layer on the pan. It should start to sizzle. Let cook for a couple of minutes, until browned, then use tongs to turn over. Continue to cook until the chicken is cooked all the way through. You can test this by slicing one of the larger pieces of chicken in half and ensuring it's hot and no longer pink in the middle.

Transfer to a cutting board and shred the chicken using 2 forks. Place on top of the salad. Add the poached egg, if using.

Serve the salad with the remaining dressing.

TIP: To seed a cucumber, slice in half lengthwise and scoop out the seeds, using a teaspoon.

SOUVLAKI CHICKEN

1 lb (454 g) chicken thigh fillets, trimmed

2 tbsp (30 ml) olive oil

2 cloves garlic, peeled and minced

Zest and juice of 1 lemon

½ tsp salt

½ tsp dried dill, or 1½ tsp (2 g) fresh, chopped

SALAD

1 head romaine lettuce, roughly shredded

1 green bell pepper, seeded and sliced

10 grape tomatoes, sliced in half

1 small red onion, thinly sliced

½ cup (75 g) crumbled feta cheese

⅓ cup (52 g) Nocellara olives (use kalamata if you prefer), sliced in half

1 cucumber, peeled, seeded and sliced into half-moons (see Tip)

½ tsp dried oregano

Heaping ¼ cup (65 g) hummus

GREEK DRESSING

½ cup (120 ml) olive oil

2 tbsp (30 ml) red wine vinegar

Zest and juice of ½ lemon

1 clove garlic, peeled and minced

½ tsp dried oregano

Pinch of salt

Pinch of freshly ground black pepper

A few fresh oregano leaves (optional)

1 poached egg (optional)

BUTTERMILK CHICKEN COBB SALAD

This is my all-time favorite crispy chicken recipe. The chicken is juicy and tender, and the coating is crispy and packed with flavor. Yep, deep-fried chicken might not be the healthiest option, but it makes one seriously tasty salad!

SERVES 4

Place the chicken in a bowl and add the buttermilk, salt, pepper and garlic salt. Mix together, cover and refrigerate for at least an hour or overnight.

In a large pan or deep fryer, heat the vegetable oil until hot. You can test by dropping in a small cube of bread; if it rises immediately to the top and starts to bubble rapidly, it's hot enough.

While the oil heats, prepare the crispy coating. In a small bowl, mix together all the coating ingredients.

Take the chicken out of the refrigerator. Lift a piece from the buttermilk and allow the excess to drip off. Dredge the chicken in the crispy coating mixture, ensuring the chicken is fully covered. Place on a tray and repeat until all the chicken is coated.

Once the oil is hot, add 5 or 6 chicken pieces at a time. You can add more or less depending on the size of your pan or fryer; just be sure not to overcrowd the chicken. Cook for 3 to 5 minutes, or until golden brown and cooked in the middle. You can check this by cutting open a piece of chicken; if it's no longer pink in the middle, it's cooked.

3 chicken breasts, sliced into long, thick strips

¾ cup (180 ml) buttermilk

½ tsp salt

¼ tsp ground white pepper

¼ tsp garlic salt

At least 4 cups (1 L) vegetable oil, for frying

CRISPY COATING

1½ cups (180 g) all-purpose flour

1 tsp salt

1 tsp freshly ground black pepper

½ tsp garlic salt

½ tsp celery salt

1 tsp dried thyme

1 tsp paprika

1 tsp baking powder

1 tsp red pepper flakes

(continued)

Transfer the chicken to a bowl lined with paper towels to drain off any excess oil. Cook and drain the remaining chicken.

Meanwhile, prepare the dressing. In a small bowl, stir together all the dressing ingredients. Refrigerate until ready to serve.

On a serving platter, arrange the lettuce, cucumber, corn, tomatoes, red onion, jalapeño and cheddar cheese, along with the crispy chicken.

Serve immediately with the ranch dressing.

HOMEMADE RANCH DRESSING

½ cup (115 g) mayonnaise

½ cup (120 ml) buttermilk

1 clove garlic, peeled and minced

1 tsp fresh lemon juice

½ tsp English mustard powder

¼ tsp onion powder

1 tbsp (4 g) fresh dill, chopped

1 tbsp (3 g) fresh chives, chopped

Pinch of salt

Pinch of freshly ground black pepper

SALAD

1 large head romaine lettuce, sliced into strips

½ cucumber, chopped into small chunks

1 cup (175 g) cooked or canned corn

10 grape tomatoes, quartered

1 small red onion, chopped into small chunks

1 jalapeño pepper, sliced

1 cup (100 g) shredded cheddar cheese

COFFEE-CRUSTED SEARED STEAK BOWL WITH SAVORY RICE AND CRUMBLED STILTON

It might sound a little strange to coat your steak in coffee grounds before frying, but they really enhance the steak, imparting a deep, rich flavor. The addition of a few herbs and spices into that coating makes the steak unforgettably good.

Serve it with Stilton-flecked savory rice salad for a seriously show-off dinner!

SERVES 4

To prepare the rice, in a medium saucepan, heat the oil over medium heat and add the red onion. Cook for 3 to 4 minutes, or until the onion starts to soften. Add the garlic, paprika, turmeric, coriander and cardamom pods. Give it a stir and allow to cook for a minute, then add the rice and hot stock. Stir and bring to a boil, then simmer gently, uncovered, for 15 to 18 minutes, or until the rice is tender. You may need to add a little more water if the pan starts to boil dry, but you shouldn't need to drain off any water at the end.

Heat a cast-iron grill pan or skillet over high heat.

(continued)

SAVORY RICE

1 tbsp (15 ml) olive oil

1 red onion, finely chopped

2 cloves garlic, peeled and minced

½ tsp paprika

½ tsp ground turmeric

½ tsp ground coriander

4 cardamom pods (see Tip on page 37)

1 cup (198 g) raw easy-cook rice

1¾ cups (420 ml) hot chicken or vegetable stock

2 cups (40 g) packed pea shoots

1 red bell pepper, seeded and sliced

1 green bell pepper, seeded and sliced

1 red onion, sliced thinly

8 grape tomatoes, chopped into small pieces

4 radishes, thinly sliced

1 cup (110 g) crumbled Stilton cheese, divided

Juice of ½ lemon

Pinch of salt

Pinch of freshly ground black pepper

On a plate, stir together the coffee, brown sugar, cumin, thyme, paprika, salt, pepper and garlic powder. Place the steaks on the plate and coat on both sides with the coffee mixture.

Brush the grill pan with the oil and add the steaks. Cook for 3 to 5 minutes on each side, depending on how well cooked you like your steak. Once cooked, transfer to a cutting board to rest for 5 to 10 minutes.

Once the rice is cooked, remove and discard the cardamom pods. Transfer to a large serving plate. Add the pea shoots, red and green bell peppers, sliced red onion, tomatoes, radishes, half of the Stilton, the lemon juice and the salt and pepper. Toss together to combine.

Slice the rested steak and place on top of the rice. Sprinkle with the parsley and remaining Stilton before serving.

TIP: Sew the cardamom pods together with undyed cotton thread so you can easily fish them out later.

COFFEE-CRUSTED STEAK

1 tbsp (5 g) packed finely ground coffee (not instant coffee)

1 tbsp (9 g) light brown muscovado sugar

1 tsp ground cumin

1 tsp dried thyme

1 tsp paprika

½ tsp salt

½ tsp freshly ground black pepper

¼ tsp garlic powder

2 fillet steaks or rib eyes, taken out of the fridge at least 30 minutes before cooking (this will help it cook more evenly)

1 tbsp (15 ml) vegetable oil

FOR SERVING

⅓ cup (20 g) chopped fresh parsley

BLT CHICKEN SALAD

The crispy bacon totally makes this salad. Cook it in the oven on a rack for ultimate crunch. I like to cook the chicken breasts on the tray underneath the bacon, so the bacon fat drips onto the chicken. A little naughty, but so, so good.

SERVES 4

Preheat the oven to 400°F (204°C).

Place the chicken breasts on a baking sheet and drizzle with the olive oil. Sprinkle with a half of the salt and pepper. Place a wire rack over the chicken, and add the bacon in a single layer so the juices from the bacon drip onto the chicken.

Bake for 15 minutes, or until the bacon is crisp. Remove the wire rack and its bacon, and set aside the bacon to cool.

Add the tomatoes to the chicken. Spoon any oil in the bottom of the pan over the tomatoes and sprinkle with the remaining salt and pepper. Place the pan back in the oven and bake for 10 to 15 minutes, or until the chicken is browned and no longer pink in the middle.

Meanwhile, place the eggs in a pan of cold water, so the water is just covering them. Bring to a boil, then simmer for 6 minutes—this will give them a slightly runny center; cook for 3 minutes more for a firmer center. Turn off the heat and transfer the eggs to a bowl of ice water. Let cool for 5 minutes, then carefully roll the eggs on a work surface to break the shells. Peel off the shells and slice the eggs in half.

Place the cooked chicken on a cutting board and cut into bite-size pieces. Slice the bacon into 1-inch (2.5-cm) pieces.

In a small bowl, stir together all the dressing ingredients.

In a large serving bowl, arrange the lettuce and pea shoots. Top with the chicken, bacon, roasted tomatoes, eggs and red onion slices.

Sprinkle with the Parmesan and serve with the dressing.

3 chicken breasts

1 tbsp (15 ml) olive oil

¼ tsp salt

¼ tsp freshly ground black pepper

8 strips bacon

12 grape tomatoes, sliced in half

4 large eggs

1 head iceberg lettuce, shredded

1 cup (20 g) packed pea shoots

½ small red onion, thinly sliced

2 tbsp (10 g) shredded Parmesan cheese

HONEY MUSTARD DRESSING

¼ cup (60 ml) olive oil

2 tsp (10 ml) white wine vinegar

3 tbsp (60 g) honey

2 tsp (8 g) Dijon mustard

Pinch of salt

Pinch of freshly ground black pepper

BULGOGI BEEF LETTUCE WRAPS

A spicy handheld salad that makes a fantastic appetizer or lunch. *Bulgogi* is a Korean dish of spicy shaved meat. The traditional marinade usually includes *gochujang* (a fermented red chile paste) and shredded Asian pear. I'm using sweet apple instead of pear, simply because it's easier to find. Jazz apples—which have a sweet-sharp flavor with a hint of pear—work particularly well.

You can use any lettuce you like for these wraps, but I'd recommend crispier lettuce leaves, such as romaine, as they hold together better.

SERVES 4

Place the steak in the freezer for 30 minutes to firm up slightly, then slice thinly against the grain, using a sharp knife. Lightly freezing the meat will help you slice it more easily.

Place the sliced steak in a large bowl and add all the bulgogi ingredients except the vegetable oil. Mix together thoroughly, then cover and refrigerate for 3 to 4 hours.

In a large skillet, heat the vegetable oil over medium-high heat. Scoop out the steak, using a slotted spoon to allow any excess sauce to drip off, then fry the steak in the hot oil. Use tongs to separate the steak slices during cooking, and cook until cooked through, about 5 minutes. Remove the steak from the heat.

Place the lettuce, underside up, on a large platter and fill with the bulgogi beef, carrot, cucumber, bell pepper and scallions. I like to keep the leaves open, like little bowls, rather than rolling them up. Sprinkle with the sesame seeds before serving.

TIP: If you want to make these wraps more substantial, you can add a spoonful of cooked rice to each wrap.

BULGOGI BEEF

2 medium sirloin steaks

2 tbsp (30 ml) soy sauce

2 tbsp (40 g) gochujang paste

1 tbsp (6 g) minced fresh ginger

2 tbsp (24 g) light brown sugar

2 tbsp (30 ml) mirin

2 cloves garlic, peeled and minced

½ tsp freshly ground black pepper

1 grated sweet apple (no need to peel)

1 tbsp (15 ml) toasted sesame oil

2 tbsp (30 ml) vegetable oil

TO ASSEMBLE

3 heads romaine or butter lettuce, leaves removed, washed and dried

1 large carrot, sliced into thin strips

⅓ cucumber, chopped into small chunks

1 red bell pepper, seeded and chopped into small chunks

3 scallions, sliced into thin strips

1 tsp sesame seeds

THAI STEAK SALAD

I'm a huge fan of Thai food—those sweet, sour, spicy flavors are so moreish! This salad has got it all, plus plenty of crunch with veggies and peanuts. We're using the dressing as a marinade for the steak and to dress the salad. I use Thai red chiles in the marinade as I like a bit of heat, but you can use whatever chiles you prefer—or leave them out entirely if you're not keen on spicy food.

SERVES 4

In a small bowl, whisk together all the dressing ingredients except the steak and vegetable oil. Pour half of the dressing over the uncooked steaks, cover and refrigerate for 1 hour. Reserve the remaining dressing for serving with the salad.

Remove the steaks from the refrigerator and discard their marinade.

In a large skillet, heat the oil over high heat and fry the steaks for 2 to 3 minutes on each side, or until browned on the outside but still a little pink in the middle.

Remove the steaks from the pan and transfer them to a cutting board to rest for a few minutes, then slice into thin slices.

Meanwhile, soak the rice noodles in boiling water for 2 to 3 minutes, or until softened. Drain and rinse in cold water.

In a large serving bowl, arrange the cucumber, carrot, red and yellow bell peppers, cabbage, scallions, noodles and all but a tablespoon (3 g) of the cilantro. Drizzle with the reserved dressing and toss together.

Top with the steak and finish with a sprinkling of chopped peanuts and the remaining cilantro.

CHILI LEMONGRASS DRESSING AND STEAK

Juice of 2 limes

2 tbsp (18 g) soft light brown sugar

2 tsp (10 ml) sesame oil

2 tsp (10 ml) Asian fish sauce

⅓ cup (13 g) finely chopped fresh cilantro

1 red Thai chile, minced, or 2 tsp (10 g) sambal oelek

2 cloves garlic, peeled and minced

2 tsp (10 g) lemongrass paste

2 small flank or sirloin steaks

1 tbsp (15 ml) vegetable oil, for frying

7 oz (198 g) dried vermicelli rice noodles

TO ASSEMBLE

½ cucumber, chopped into small chunks

1 medium carrot, peeled and sliced into matchsticks

1 red bell pepper, seeded and thinly sliced

1 yellow bell pepper, seeded and thinly sliced

½ green cabbage, sliced into thin strips (about 18 oz [510 g] sliced)

3 scallions, chopped

⅓ cup (6 g) chopped fresh cilantro, divided

2 tbsp (18 g) chopped peanuts

CHIMICHURRI STEAK SALAD

An Argentinean spin on a steak salad—this meal is vibrant, zingy and delicious! I like to chop the ingredients for my chimichurri, but you can use a small food processor if you'd like it smoother.

You could even add a little cooked quinoa or rice, if you want to bulk out this dish for a more filling meal.

SERVES 4

Heat a cast-iron grill pan or skillet over high heat.

Place the steaks on a cutting board and drizzle with the oil, then sprinkle them with the salt and black pepper. Rub in the oil and seasonings with your hands to coat on both sides.

Cook the steaks for 3 to 5 minutes on each side, depending on how well cooked you like your steaks. Once cooked, transfer to a cutting board to rest for 5 to 10 minutes.

Meanwhile, prepare the chimichurri. In a small bowl, stir together all the chimichurri ingredients. Allow to sit for a few minutes while you finish the rest of the salad.

Assemble the salad. On a serving platter, arrange the baby salad leaves, tomatoes, radishes, avocado, red onion, cucumber and flatbreads.

Top with the cooked steak, then drizzle with most of the chimichurri. Nestle a small dollop of the sour cream into the platter and drizzle a little more chimichurri on top before serving.

STEAK

2 sirloin steaks (about 7 oz [198 g] each)

1½ tbsp (23 ml) vegetable oil

¼ tsp salt

¼ tsp freshly ground black pepper

CHIMICHURRI

1 cup (60 g) packed fresh parsley, chopped very finely

½ tsp red pepper flakes, chopped very finely

6 tbsp (90 ml) olive oil

2 cloves garlic, peeled and minced

¼ tsp salt

¼ tsp freshly ground black pepper

¼ tsp dried oregano

1 tbsp (15 ml) fresh lemon juice

1 tsp red wine vinegar

SALAD

3 cups (90 g) packed baby salad leaves

10 grape tomatoes, sliced in half

2 radishes, thinly sliced

1 avocado, peeled, pitted and chopped into small chunks

½ red onion, sliced thinly

½ cucumber, sliced

2 flatbreads, toasted and sliced into large wedges

2 tbsp (30 g) sour cream

PILED-HIGH CURED MEAT DELI BOARD

A no-cook party platter, piled high with a selection of goodies that will make your guests feel truly pampered. It might seem a little strange to refer to a deli board as a salad, but it contains lots of elements of a really good salad, so I'm going with it!

I love to prepare a board like this for Christmas as a starter, to keep everyone satisfied while I'm rushing around the kitchen. It's even better when you can hand over all the ingredients to the kids and let them make it up.

SERVES 4

On a large platter or serving board, arrange the antipasto meats in little piles.

Place the hummus in a small bowl and the Greek mixed olives in a second bowl, and set on the board along with the jar of fig preserve.

Arrange the breadsticks, stuffed mini peppers, endive leaves, sun-dried tomatoes, grapes, crackers, feta, Parmigiano-Reggiano, apricots and pistachios on the board. Fill any spaces with the baby salad leaves.

To serve, drizzle the hummus with olive oil and sprinkle with a pinch of black pepper.

Sprinkle the parsley on the hummus and feta.

6 oz (170 g) mixed antipasto meats, such as prosciutto, coppa and Milano salami

7 oz (198 g) hummus

1 cup (155 g) Greek mixed olives with garlic and herbs (available at the deli counter)

1 small jar fig preserve/spread

2 oz (57 g) mini grissini breadsticks

6 to 8 cream cheese–stuffed mini peppers (available at the deli counter)

1 red endive, separated into individual leaves

½ cup (55 g) oil-packed sun-dried tomatoes

Large bunch of red seedless grapes

8 to 12 mixed crackers

½ cup (75 g) crumbled feta cheese

1 (7-oz [198-g]) block Parmigiano-Reggiano cheese, roughly broken into large chunks

3 fresh apricots, sliced in half and pitted

¼ cup (30 g) pistachios

1 cup (30 g) packed baby salad leaves

TO SERVE

2 tbsp (30 ml) olive oil

Good pinch of freshly ground black pepper

⅓ cup (20 g) chopped fresh parsley

ROASTED TOMATO, CHORIZO AND RICE SALAD

Roasting tomatoes in the oven with garlic and olive oil adds a level of flavor and sweetness like no other. That rich, sweet taste works perfectly with the salty chorizo. I cook my chorizo in the oven with the tomatoes to save on cleanup, but you can always fry it, if you prefer.

A simple balsamic dressing finishes off the dish perfectly.

SERVES 4

Preheat the oven to 425°F (218°C). Line a baking sheet with parchment paper.

In a bowl, combine the tomatoes with the garlic, oil, salt and pepper and toss together. Transfer to the prepared baking sheet and roast for 15 minutes. If you're using small tomatoes, roast for just 5 to 6 minutes.

Add the asparagus to the pan with the tomatoes, and move it around to coat it with some of the oil. Then, add the sliced chorizo and place the pan back in the oven to roast for an additional 10 minutes, or until the tomatoes and asparagus are lightly browned. Remove from the oven.

In a small bowl, whisk together all the dressing ingredients.

In a bowl, combine the arugula, baby spinach, rice and red onion, then pour half of the dressing over them and toss together.

Arrange the roasted tomatoes, asparagus and chorizo on top (see Tips).

Serve with the remaining dressing.

TIPS: You can use whole tomatoes still on the vine, if you prefer. In this case, drizzle with the oil, rather than tossing to coat, to prevent their detaching from the vine.

You can spoon the garlic and oil from the baking sheet over the salad, too, for even more flavor.

1 lb (454 g) mixed-color tomatoes, sliced in half (see Tips)

3 cloves garlic, peeled and sliced

2 tbsp (30 ml) olive oil

½ tsp salt

¼ tsp freshly ground black pepper

8 oz (226 g) asparagus, ends trimmed

4 oz (113 g) chorizo, thickly sliced

2 cups (50 g) packed baby arugula

2 cups (60 g) packed baby spinach leaves

2 cups (333 g) cooked basmati and wild rice blend (about ⅔ cup [130 g] raw)

1 small red onion, sliced

BALSAMIC DRESSING

¼ cup (60 ml) good-quality balsamic vinegar

3 tbsp (45 ml) olive oil

¼ tsp salt

¼ tsp freshly ground black pepper

CHORIZO AND LIMA BEAN SALAD

Spicy chorizo, creamy lima beans, fresh pea shoots and tangy feta come together to make this a salad to really tickle those taste buds!

I prefer this salad with the chorizo and lima beans served warm, but it still tastes great served cold if you're taking it into work for lunch.

SERVES 4

In a medium skillet, heat the oil over medium-high heat.

Add the chorizo and cook for 2 to 3 minutes, or until the chorizo starts to brown at the edges and releases its oils.

Add the lima beans, salt and black pepper and cook, stirring occasionally, for 2 to 3 minutes, or until the beans are hot throughout. Turn off the heat.

In a small bowl, stir together all the dressing ingredients.

In a large serving bowl, combine the pea shoots, tomatoes, roasted peppers and red onion. Top with the chorizo and lima beans and toss together.

Sprinkle with the crumbled feta and parsley and serve with the dressing.

I tsp vegetable oil

4 oz (113 g) chorizo, roughly chopped

1 (14-oz [397-g]) can white lima beans (butterbeans), drained and rinsed

¼ tsp salt

¼ tsp freshly ground black pepper

3 cups (60 g) packed pea shoots

1 cup (110 g) oil-packed sun-dried tomatoes, roughly chopped

2 roasted peppers from a jar, roughly chopped

1 red onion, thinly sliced

½ cup (75 g) crumbled feta cheese

1 tbsp (4 g) finely chopped parsley

ITALIAN HERB DRESSING

3 tbsp (45 ml) olive oil

2 tbsp (30 ml) red wine vinegar

¼ tsp salt

¼ tsp freshly ground black pepper

½ clove garlic, peeled and minced

½ tsp light brown sugar

1½ tsp (2 g) dried oregano

½ tsp dried thyme

WARM BACON AND PEA SALAD WITH LEMON DRESSING

Some might say eight slices of bacon is a lot for a pea salad, but my husband would probably ask me to double that amount!

The saltiness of the bacon works so well with the sweetness of the peas and the crunch of the pea shoots.

This dish is best served warm. It also makes a great side for chicken or white fish.

SERVES 4 AS A SIDE DISH

In a large skillet, heat the oil over high heat.

Add the bacon and cook, stirring often, until lightly browned and golden, about 5 minutes.

Add the onion and lower the heat to medium. Cook, stirring often, for 3 minutes, until the onion starts to soften.

Meanwhile, prepare the dressing. In a small bowl, stir together all the dressing ingredients.

Add the peas, salt and pepper to the bacon and continue to cook, stirring occasionally, for 4 to 5 minutes, or until the peas are hot through.

Turn off the heat and add the pea shoots to the pan. Toss together to coat the pea shoots with the oil and wilt them slightly.

Transfer to a serving bowl and top with the Parmesan. Serve with the dressing.

2 tbsp (30 ml) vegetable oil

8 strips bacon, chopped into small pieces

1 red onion, sliced

2 cups (300 g) fresh peas or frozen petits pois (no need to thaw)

¼ tsp salt

¼ tsp freshly ground black pepper

2 cups (40 g) packed pea shoots

2 tbsp (10 g) shredded Parmesan cheese

LEMON DRESSING

Juice of 1 lemon

3 tbsp (45 ml) olive oil

¼ tsp salt

¼ tsp freshly ground black pepper

½ clove garlic, peeled and minced

½ tsp light brown sugar

SHREDDED BRUSSELS SPROUT AND BACON SALAD

I'm a Brussels sprouts lover. I'll eat them whenever they're available, boiled, roasted, steamed—just give me the sprouts.

Chris will eat them over the Christmas period, and the kids will agree to eat two each on Christmas day . . .

. . . unless I make this salad! A sprout salad for non-sprout-lovers! You can't beat a bit of bacon to up everyone's sprout intake.

SERVES 4

Peel the outer leaves from the Brussels sprouts, and chop off and discard the ends of the stalks. Slice the sprouts very thinly.

In a large skillet, melt the butter over medium-high heat. Add the garlic and sauté for 30 seconds, then add the sliced sprouts and a good pinch of salt and pepper. Sauté the sprouts, tossing them with the garlic butter to coat, for 1 to 2 minutes, until they are warmed through yet still vibrantly green. Transfer to a serving bowl. Add the Parmesan to the sprouts and toss to incorporate.

In a small bowl, stir together all the dressing ingredients. Pour half of the dressing over the sprouts.

Sprinkle the bacon, fried onions and parsley on top and serve with the remaining dressing.

18 oz (510 g) Brussels sprouts

2 tbsp (28 g) unsalted butter

2 cloves garlic, peeled and minced

Good pinch of salt

Good pinch of freshly ground black pepper

¼ cup (20 g) shredded Parmesan cheese

HONEY MUSTARD DRESSING

¼ cup (60 ml) olive oil

2 tsp (10 ml) white wine vinegar

3 tbsp (60 g) honey

2 tsp (8 g) Dijon mustard

Pinch of salt

Pinch of freshly ground black pepper

6 strips cooked bacon, finely chopped

2 tbsp (26 g) crunchy fried onions (available ready-made)

1 tbsp (4 g) finely chopped fresh parsley

PANFRIED IBERICO PORK AND MANCHEGO SALAD

I first tasted the delights of Iberico pork with quince and Manchego in Barcelona when we were there for my husband's birthday. We sat outside a little street café with chilled white wine in oversize glasses and marveled over every morsel.

The quince was served in little sticky cubes that tasted amazing with the saltiness of the pork and Manchego.

This salad is inspired by that meal. Served with a quince dressing, tender mâche and sweet-ripe figs, this is a luxury lunch that also makes an impressive dinner party starter.

Ensure the lettuce, figs and apple are at room temperature for maximum flavor.

SERVES 4

Heat a medium-size skillet over high heat.

Place the pork on a cutting board and rub the oil, salt and pepper into the shoulder steak. Place in the hot pan and cook for 2 to 3 minutes on each side, or until golden and cooked through.

Transfer from the pan to a clean cutting board to rest while you prepare the salad dressing.

In a bowl, mash the quince paste with a fork. Add the oil, a drizzle at a time, and mix it into the paste, using the fork, until no lumps remain. Stir in the vinegar, water, honey, salt and pepper until incorporated.

Divide the mâche, figs and apple among 4 small plates.

Chop the pork into small cubes and add to the plates. Top with the crumbled Manchego and toasted almonds.

Drizzle with the dressing before serving.

4 oz (113 g) Iberico pork shoulder steak

1 tbsp (15 ml) vegetable oil

½ tsp salt

½ tsp freshly ground black pepper

2 cups (40 g) packed mâche

4 figs, quartered

1 sweet apple, cored and sliced into small cubes (mix with 1 tsp of fresh lemon juice to prevent browning after slicing)

2 oz (57 g) Manchego cheese, crumbled

2 tbsp (14 g) flaked almonds, toasted

QUINCE DRESSING

3 tbsp (54 g) quince paste

3 tbsp (45 ml) olive oil

1 tbsp (15 ml) red wine vinegar

1 tbsp (15 ml) water

1 tsp honey

¼ tsp salt

¼ tsp freshly ground black pepper

STICKY PORK BELLY WITH CRUNCHY SALAD

The three cooking processes for this pork make it melt in the mouth and seriously addictive. First, it's cooked slowly in seasoned stock until tender. Then, it's fried until golden and lightly crisped, then it's bubbled up in a sweet-salty-sticky sauce. It's one of my favorite Asian dishes that I've been cooking for years, and a favorite with my blog readers, too.

This makes a luxurious topping to a crunchy salad—but it is difficult not to eat half the pork before serving it!

SERVES 4

In a large, lidded saucepan, combine all the pork ingredients. Bring to a boil, then cover, lower the heat and simmer for 2 hours.

Turn off the heat and drain the pork. You can reserve the liquid if you like (great for a Chinese noodle soup). Chop the pork into bite-size chunks.

In a skillet, heat 1 tablespoon (15 ml) of the oil over high heat. Sprinkle the pork with the salt and pepper and add to the pan. Fry, turning often, for 4 to 5 minutes, or until golden (be careful, it may spit).

Meanwhile, in a small bowl, stir together the remaining glaze ingredients.

When the pork is golden, pour the glaze over the pork and continue to cook until the pork looks dark and sticky, about 2 minutes. Turn off the heat and transfer the pork to a bowl to stop the caramelization process.

(continued)

SLOW-COOKED PORK BELLY

2.2 lb (1 kg) rindless pork belly slices, chopped in half (each piece about 2½" [6.5-cm] long)

1 quart (1 L) hot chicken or vegetable stock

1 tsp minced fresh ginger

3 cloves garlic, peeled and chopped in half

1 tbsp (15 ml) mirin

1 tbsp (13 g) superfine sugar

GLAZE

2 tbsp (30 ml) vegetable oil, divided

Pinch of salt

Pinch of freshly ground black pepper

1 tsp minced fresh ginger

1 red chile, finely chopped

2 tbsp (40 g) honey

2 tbsp (18 g) light brown sugar

3 tbsp (45 ml) dark soy sauce

1 tsp lemongrass paste

For the dressing, in a small bowl, stir together all the dressing ingredients.

Arrange the green and red cabbage, carrot, cucumber, water chestnuts and bean sprouts equally among 4 plates.

Spoon the sticky pork on top and sprinkle with the cashews. Serve with the dressing.

LIGHT CHILI DRESSING

2 tbsp (30 ml) olive oil

1 tbsp (20 g) sweet chili sauce

1 tbsp (15 ml) dark soy sauce

Juice of ½ lime

1 tsp superfine sugar

SALAD

1 head sweetheart cabbage, finely sliced (about 17 oz [482 g] sliced)

¼ red cabbage, finely sliced (about 11 oz [312 g] sliced)

1 carrot, peeled, then sliced into strips, using a vegetable peeler

1 mini cucumber, sliced

1 (8-oz [227-g]) can sliced water chestnuts, drained

1 packed cup (100 g) bean sprouts (fresh is better, but from a can, drained, is fine)

¼ cup (35 g) cashews, toasted and roughly chopped

HAM HOCK, SPRING PEA, ZUCCHINI AND ASPARAGUS SALAD

Ham hock is a cheap cut of meat from the lower leg of the pig. You can often buy it ready cooked and shredded. It's deliciously tender when cooked slowly, and works peculiarly well with green vegetables, such as asparagus and snap peas.

A tangy lemon and mustard dressing cuts through these rich flavors perfectly.

SERVES 4

Heat a large cast-iron grill pan over high heat.

In a small bowl, stir together the oil, salt and pepper. Brush half on both sides of the ciabatta slices.

Drizzle the remaining seasoned oil over the asparagus and zucchini ribbons.

Place the ciabatta and asparagus on the grill pan and cook for 1 to 2 minutes on each side, or until slightly browned. Remove from the pan and slice the toasted ciabatta into bite-size chunks.

Place the zucchini ribbons on the pan and cook for 30 to 60 seconds, or until grill lines appear; no need to turn. Remove from the pan.

In a small bowl, whisk together all the dressing ingredients.

On a serving platter, arrange the pea shoots and salad leaves and top with the shredded ham, toasted ciabatta, asparagus, zucchini, snap peas and pine nuts.

Drizzle with the dressing before serving.

3 tbsp (45 ml) olive oil

¼ tsp salt

¼ tsp freshly ground black pepper

4 thick slices ciabatta bread

4 oz (113 g) asparagus, ends trimmed

1 large zucchini, shaved into ribbons, using a vegetable peeler

2 cups (40 g) packed pea shoots

2 cups (60 g) packed baby salad leaves

1 cup (150 g) shredded cooked ham hock

1½ cups (128 g) fresh snap peas—half shelled, half sliced in half lengthwise

¼ cup (34 g) pine nuts, toasted

LEMON AND MUSTARD DRESSING

⅓ cup (80 ml) olive oil

Juice of ½ lemon

1 tsp light brown sugar

1 tbsp (11 g) whole-grain mustard

½ tsp Dijon mustard

Pinch of salt

Pinch of freshly ground black pepper

SHREDDED HAM HOCK SALAD WITH SOFT-BOILED EGGS AND HONEY MUSTARD DRESSING

It took me 36 years to figure out how to peel an egg without taking half the egg white with it! The secret is a short spell in ice water right after cooking. When they're cooked for just six minutes, you're left with a slightly runny center that begs to be dipped into!

Served with baby new potatoes and shredded ham hock, this salad is substantial enough for dinner.

SERVES 4

Place the potatoes in a saucepan and cover with cold water. Bring to a boil, then simmer for 15 minutes until tender, adding the peas to the water at the 12-minute point. Drain and set aside.

Meanwhile, place the eggs in a saucepan of cold water, so the water is just covering them. Bring to a boil, then simmer for 6 minutes—this will give a slightly runny center; cook for 3 minutes more for a firm center.

Turn off the heat and transfer the eggs to a bowl of ice water. Let cool for 5 minutes, then carefully roll the eggs on a work surface to break the shells. Peel off the shells and slice the eggs in half.

In a small bowl, whisk together all the dressing ingredients.

On a serving dish, create a bed of the watercress and top with the potatoes, peas, eggs, shredded ham and sliced radishes.

Sprinkle with the chopped chives and drizzle with the dressing before serving.

1 lb (454 g) baby new potatoes, halved

1 cup (150 g) freshly shelled peas

4 large eggs

2 cups (40 g) packed watercress

1 cup (150 g) shredded cooked ham hock

3 radishes, thinly sliced

1/3 cup (6 g) chopped fresh chives

HONEY MUSTARD DRESSING

1/4 cup (60 ml) olive oil

2 tsp (10 ml) white wine vinegar

2 tbsp (40 g) honey

2 tsp (8 g) Dijon mustard

Pinch of salt

Pinch of freshly ground black pepper

PROSCIUTTO AND PEACH SALAD WITH FIGS

This no-cook, deliciously simple lunch tastes at its absolute best during summer, when peaches and figs are big and juicy. You'll get maximum flavor from these fruits if they're served at room temperature, rather than straight from the refrigerator.

Use fresh thyme in the dressing for a beautifully aromatic finish.

SERVES 4

On a serving plate, arrange the baby salad leaves. Nestle in slices of prosciutto, peaches, figs and Brie.

In a small bowl, whisk together all the dressing ingredients.

Drizzle the salad with the dressing and sprinkle with the chopped walnuts before serving.

TIP: If your peaches and figs are a little underripe, you can dust slices of them with a little brown sugar and grill for a couple of minutes to sweeten them right up.

3 cups (90 g) packed baby salad leaves

3 oz (85 g) prosciutto

3 ripe peaches, sliced

4 figs, quartered

8 oz (227 g) Brie cheese, sliced into small chunks

¼ cup (32 g) roughly chopped walnuts

HONEY THYME DRESSING

¼ cup (60 ml) olive oil

Juice of ½ lemon

3 tbsp (60 g) honey

2 tsp (8 g) Dijon mustard

1 tbsp (3 g) chopped thyme leaves

Pinch of salt

Pinch of freshly ground black pepper

CHINESE DUCK SALAD WITH PLUMS

I've tried numerous methods to make crispy duck in the oven, and this one is by far the quickest and easiest. No brining or blanching, but still full of flavor, with juicy flesh and crispy skin.

Roasted plums add a lovely element of sweetness, and a simple salad of leaves, cucumber and scallions adds freshness and vibrancy.

SERVES 6

Preheat the oven to 300°F (149°C). Place a wire rack inside a large roasting pan.

Pat down the duck with paper towels to ensure the skin is dry. Score the skin of the duck on the breast side in a crisscross pattern with a sharp knife. Try not to pierce the flesh.

Place the duck, breast side up, on the rack in the roasting pan. Season with salt, pepper and Chinese five-spice powder, and roast for 3 hours and 20 minutes, turning over the duck every hour (I use a clean kitchen towel in each hand to do this). Turning the duck helps redistribute the fat and results in a lovely crisp skin.

Then, add the plums to the wire rack and brush them a little with the oil from the bottom of the pan.

Roast for an additional 30 minutes, until the duck is dark brown and the plums are soft.

Meanwhile, prepare the dressing. In a small bowl, whisk together all the dressing ingredients. You can leave out the water if you like a very thick sauce or add a little more water if you want it more pourable.

Once cooked, remove the duck from the oven. Let it rest for 10 minutes, then transfer to a large cutting board and use 2 forks to shred the meat.

On a large serving plate, arrange the micro herbs, purslane and cucumber.

Top with the shredded duck and roasted plums.

Sprinkle with the scallions and serve with the dressing.

CHINESE DUCK
1 duck (about 4½ lb [2 kg]), innards removed

½ tsp salt

½ tsp freshly ground black pepper

1 tsp Chinese five-spice powder

6 plums, sliced in half and pitted

QUICK ASIAN DRESSING
1 tbsp (15 ml) sesame oil

1 tbsp (15 ml) sriracha

¼ cup (60 ml) hoisin sauce

1 tbsp (15 ml) water (optional)

1 small clove garlic, peeled and minced

Pinch of ground ginger

Pinch of salt

Pinch of freshly ground black pepper

SALAD
2 cups (50 g) Asian micro herbs (such as cilantro, red radish and pea shoots)

2 packed cups (60 g) purslane leaves or baby spinach

1 cucumber, peeled, seeded and sliced into long strips, using a vegetable peeler

4 scallions, sliced into thin strips

LAMB AND ORANGE SALAD

You can cook this lamb in the oven or a slow cooker and have it ready for a light evening meal with minimal prep. The salad is really simple, and the orange works great to complement and cut through the richness of the meat.

You can cook the lamb specifically for this salad, or, as I often do, cook it for dinner with vegetables and potatoes, then save some of the lamb the next day for this salad.

SERVES 6

Preheat the oven to 300°F (149°C).

In a large, lidded roasting pan, heat the oil over high heat. Pat the lamb dry with paper towels and sprinkle all over with salt and pepper. Place the lamb in the pan and sear on all sides, for 6 to 8 minutes.

Lower the heat and add the red pepper flakes, tomato paste, oregano, brown sugar, stock and garlic. Stir and bring to a boil.

Turn off the heat. Place the lid on the pan and transfer it to the oven to roast for 3 hours, or until tender. Alternatively, you can transfer to a slow cooker and cook for 4 to 5 hours on HIGH or 6 to 8 hours on LOW. Check once or twice during the last hour of cooking and top up with a little hot water, if needed.

Once cooked, transfer the lamb from the pan to a cutting board. Shred, using 2 forks.

Meanwhile, prepare the salad. Use a sharp knife to remove the skin from the oranges. Over a bowl, cut the oranges into segments, reserving any juice that catches in the bowl.

On a large plate, arrange the baby salad leaves, orange segments and shredded beets. Top with the shredded lamb.

Drizzle a little of the cooking juices over the lamb along with any reserved orange juice. Serve the salad with toasted flatbreads.

LAMB

2 tbsp (30 ml) vegetable oil

About 4½ lb (2 kg) lamb shoulder

½ tsp salt

½ tsp freshly ground black pepper

1 tsp red pepper flakes

1 tbsp (20 g) tomato paste

1 tsp dried oregano

1 tbsp (9 g) light brown sugar

3 cups (720 ml) chicken or lamb stock

2 cloves garlic, sliced in half (no need to peel)

SALAD

3 oranges

3 cups (90 g) baby salad leaves

½ cup (75 g) shredded cooked beets

TO SERVE

Toasted flatbreads

FILLING FISH AND SEAFOOD

It took me a long time to really enjoy fish and seafood. I think it's so true that your palate really does change over time.

When I was little, the only fish I would eat were fish sticks (or fish fingers, as we call them in England), or a strange concoction of pasta, tuna, ketchup and cheese that sounds pretty awful now!

By the time I got to college, I realized I didn't want to be a fussy eater, but I did want to enjoy everything I ate. So, I started trying more things I *thought* I didn't like.

Fish and seafood, such as trout, shrimp, mussels and crab, were all on the list (as well as a few nonfishy things, such as mushrooms and olives). Over time, I've eaten them served in different ways, and now I love them all. Okay, apart from the olives. That's still a work in progress.

I hope you enjoy these fish and seafood salads, and if you're not a big seafood fan, maybe one of these recipes will sway you!

The Baja Fish Taco Bowl (page 82) and the Coconut Shrimp Salad with Asian Slaw (page 89) are my favorites from this section. Partly because they taste so good, but also because they remind me of memories I hold dear.

HAWAIIAN SALMON SALAD

This is the best way to cook salmon in my opinion! Marinate it, then throw it on a grill pan along with some chunky slices of pineapple. The marinade in this recipe has a dual purpose: flavoring the salmon and using as a salad dressing.

You could also cook it on the barbecue if the weather's good. This salad makes a lovely al fresco dinner on a warm summer evening.

SERVES 2

In a small bowl, stir together all the salmon ingredients, except the salmon, until combined.

Place the salmon in a separate bowl and pour half of the marinade over it. Cover and refrigerate for 30 minutes. Cover and refrigerate the rest of the marinade to reserve it for the salad dressing.

Heat a cast-iron grill pan over medium to high heat and brush with oil. Place the ear of corn on the pan and cook, turning regularly, for 7 to 10 minutes, or until lightly charred, and add the baby peppers for the last 5 minutes, turning once until lightly cooked.

Remove the corn and peppers from the pan. Set aside to cool for a few minutes, then carefully slice off the corn kernels.

Sprinkle the brown sugar on the pineapple slices, then cook on the grill pan, turning once, for 2 to 3 minutes, or until lightly charred. Remove from the pan and sprinkle with the red pepper flakes.

Remove the salmon from the marinade and place on the grill pan, skin side down. Brush the fillets with a little of the marinade that the salmon was in, then discard the rest of this marinade. Cook for 3 to 4 minutes on each side, or until cooked throughout. Remove from the pan.

On a serving plate, arrange the lettuce, avocado, red onion and tomatoes. Top with the grilled salmon, corn, baby peppers and pineapple.

Sprinkle with the cilantro and serve with the reserved salad dressing.

SALMON

2 tbsp (30 ml) olive oil

5 tbsp (75 ml) pineapple juice

1 tsp honey

1 tbsp (20 g) tomato paste

1 tbsp (15 ml) soy sauce

½ tsp minced fresh ginger

1 clove garlic, peeled and minced

Pinch of freshly ground black pepper

Pinch of salt

2 salmon fillets

SALAD

Oil, for the pan

1 ear of corn

2 sweet baby peppers, sliced in half and seeded

2 tbsp (18 g) light brown sugar

4 large slices pineapple

Pinch of red pepper flakes

1 head romaine lettuce, sliced

1 avocado, peeled, pitted and sliced

½ small red onion, finely chopped

10 grape tomatoes, sliced in half

⅓ cup (13 g) chopped fresh cilantro

SMOKED MACKEREL NIÇOISE

Although a classic niçoise is usually made with tuna, smoked mackerel makes a tasty change. You could also try poached trout or salmon for a more delicate flavor.

Serve the salad with a light lemon and mustard dressing (totally delicious on those baby new potatoes!).

SERVES 4

Place the potatoes in a pan of salted cold water. Bring to a boil and simmer for 15 minutes, or until tender. Drain and set aside.

Place the green beans in a pan of cold water, bring to a boil and simmer for 5 minutes. Drain and run under cold water.

Place the eggs in a pan of cold water, so the water is just covering the eggs. Bring to a boil, then simmer for 6 minutes—this will give a slightly runny center; cook for 3 minutes more for a firmer center. Turn off the heat and transfer the eggs to a bowl of ice water. Let cool for 5 minutes, then carefully roll the eggs on a work surface to break the shells. Peel off the shells and slice the eggs into quarters.

Prepare the dressing. In a small bowl, whisk together all the dressing ingredients.

Arrange the lettuce leaves, cucumber, tomatoes, green beans, potatoes, eggs, mackerel and olives in 4 bowls.

Drizzle with the dressing and serve.

8 oz (227 g) baby new potatoes, quartered

8 oz (227 g) green beans

4 large eggs

2 heads baby gem lettuce, leaves separated and washed

½ cucumber, sliced in half lengthwise, seeded and sliced into half-moons

8 grape tomatoes, quartered

7 oz (198 g) smoked mackerel, lightly shredded with a fork

¼ cup (39 g) mixed olives

LEMON AND MUSTARD DRESSING

⅓ cup (80 ml) olive oil

Juice of ½ lemon

1 tsp light brown sugar

1 tbsp (11 g) whole-grain mustard

½ tsp Dijon mustard

Pinch of salt

Pinch of freshly ground black pepper

BLACKENED SALMON CITRUS SALAD WITH AVOCADO DRESSING

This Cajun spice—coated salmon has got a real spicy kick. I like to cook up extra salmon and flake it for lunch the next day. Ruby Red grapefruits look vibrantly beautiful in this salad, but use whatever citrus fruits you have on hand. Blood oranges are also a fantastic addition when they're in season.

The citrus fruit can be a little tricky to slice thinly, so make sure you've got a sharp knife and a well-secured cutting board.

SERVES 4

Brush the salmon on both sides, using 1 tablespoon (15 ml) of the oil. Mix together the Cajun seasoning and oregano and sprinkle onto the salmon to fully coat.

In a skillet, heat the remaining tablespoon (15 ml) of the oil over medium heat and fry the salmon for 3 to 4 minutes on each side, or until cooked through.

Meanwhile, use a sharp knife to remove the skin from the grapefruit, clementines and orange. Slice the fruits into thin slices.

Prepare the dressing. In a blender, combine all the dressing ingredients and blend until smooth. Transfer to a small pitcher or bottle.

On a serving plate, combine the baby salad and radicchio leaves. Arrange the sliced fruit on top and add the salmon fillets.

Drizzle with a little of the dressing and serve the salad with the rest of the dressing on the side.

4 skinless salmon fillets

2 tbsp (30 ml) vegetable oil, divided

3 tbsp (23 g) Cajun seasoning

1 tsp dried oregano

1 Ruby Red grapefruit

2 clementines

1 orange

3 cups (90 g) packed baby salad leaves

½ small head radicchio, sliced into thin strips

AVOCADO DRESSING

1 ripe avocado, peeled and pitted

1 cup (40 g) packed fresh cilantro, chopped

1 tsp lime juice

1 clove garlic, peeled

2 tbsp (28 g) mayonnaise

2 tbsp (30 g) sour cream

2 tbsp (10 g) shredded Parmesan cheese

½ tsp salt

Pinch of freshly ground black pepper

½ cup (120 ml) water

SALMON SUSHI SALAD

I've tried my hand at making homemade sushi rolls and nigiri and ended up with my hands and kitchen covered in sticky rice, and with an aching back from hunching over the work surface.

So, I'm totally going down the cheffy-sounding "deconstructed" route with this one.

This salad is delicious, with all those sushi flavors, plus extra veggies for crunch and color.

It makes a filling lunch for four people, but it will stretch to six if you're after a lighter meal.

SERVES 4

Rinse the sushi rice under cold water and place in a saucepan. Add the cold water. Bring to a boil, cover, then lower the heat to low and cook for 10 minutes. Turn off the heat and leave, covered, for 30 minutes.

After 30 minutes, remove the lid and let the rice cool to room temperature, then gently stir the rice vinegar, sugar and salt into the rice.

In a small bowl, whisk together all the dressing ingredients.

Divide the rice among 4 bowls and top with the salmon, cucumber, shredded beet, carrot, edamame and radish slices.

Add a few nori strips to each bowl, reserving the rest for serving. Place a few slices of sushi ginger in each bowl and sprinkle with sesame seeds and shichimi togarashi.

Serve with the dressing and extra nori strips.

2 cups (350 g) uncooked sushi rice

3 cups cold water

2 tbsp (30 ml) rice vinegar

1 tbsp (15 g) sugar

¼ tsp salt

7 oz (198 g) smoked salmon, cut into 1" (2.5-cm) pieces

½ cucumber, seeded and sliced into thin strips

1 large cooked beet, peeled and shredded

1 large carrot, peeled and sliced into thin strips

1 cup (150 g) cooked edamame

4 radishes, thinly sliced

2 sheets nori seaweed, cut into ⅜" (1-cm) strips or small triangles

1 oz (28 g) pickled sushi ginger

1 tsp mixed black and white sesame seeds

1 tsp shichimi togarashi (see Note on page 16)

SOY SAUCE AND GINGER DRESSING

1 tbsp (15 ml) sesame oil

2 tbsp (30 ml) olive oil

2 tbsp (30 ml) soy sauce

1 tsp minced fresh ginger

1 clove garlic, peeled and minced

Pinch of freshly ground black pepper

BAJA FISH TACO BOWL

Crispy seasoned fish, served with lots of fresh veggies and a creamy cilantro lime dressing. This gorgeous dish reminds me of our family road trip down the California coast a few years ago. I'm pretty sure I ate fish tacos at least every other day! You can swap out the cod for other fish, but it's a good idea to stick to a firm-fleshed white fish, such as halibut or haddock.

SERVES 4

In a small bowl, stir together all the dressing ingredients. Cover and place in the refrigerator.

In a large, deep skillet, heat around 2 inches (5 cm) of vegetable oil over medium-high heat, until hot. Preheat the oven to 150°F (65°C) to keep the fish warm once cooked.

In a large bowl, stir together the salt, black pepper, white pepper, garlic salt, flour, baking powder, oregano, paprika and chili powder, then stir in the beer to create a thick batter.

Dredge each of the fish strips in the batter and place carefully in the hot oil. You will probably need to work in 2 or 3 batches. Turn once and cook until golden, for 3 to 4 minutes. Once cooked, remove from the oil with a slotted spoon, transfer to a baking sheet and place in the oven to keep warm. Repeat with the rest of the fish.

Divide the rice between 4 bowls, top with the baby salad leaves, crispy fish, corn, mixed beans, avocado, red cabbage, red onion and tomatoes.

Drizzle with the dressing and top with lime wedges before serving.

CREAMY CILANTRO LIME DRESSING

5 tbsp (75 g) Greek yogurt

1 tsp honey

Pinch of salt

½ clove garlic, peeled and minced

1 tsp fresh lime juice

3 tbsp (8 g) finely chopped fresh cilantro

1 tbsp (15 ml) water

FISH

Vegetable oil, for frying

1 tsp salt

1 tsp freshly ground black pepper

¼ tsp ground white pepper

½ tsp garlic salt

1½ cups (188 g) all-purpose flour

1 tsp baking powder

1 tsp dried oregano

1 tsp paprika

1 tsp chili powder

1½ cups (360 ml) beer

4 cod fillets, sliced into thick strips

SALAD

1½ cups (250 g) cooked rice (about ½ cup [99 g] raw), warm or cold

3 cups (90 g) packed baby salad leaves

1 cup (175 g) cooked or canned corn

1 (14-oz [397-g]) can mixed beans, drained and rinsed

1 ripe avocado, peeled, pitted and chopped into small chunks

¼ red cabbage, finely chopped (about 11 oz [312 g] chopped)

½ red onion, finely sliced

10 cherry tomatoes, sliced in half

Lime wedges, for serving

SPICY TROPICAL SHRIMP SALAD

A spicy shrimp salad served with a tropical-style chopped salsa, bursting with color. I love this for lunch to brighten up any day.

The kiwi berries make such a cute addition, but if you can't find them, regular kiwifruit is fine.

SERVES 4

In a skillet, heat the oil over medium-high heat. Add the shrimp and cook, stirring occasionally, for 2 minutes, or until just starting to turn pink.

Lower the heat to medium and add the garlic, salt, black pepper, paprika and red pepper flakes. Stir to coat and cook for an additional 2 to 3 minutes, or until lightly browned. Turn off the heat.

In a small bowl, stir together all the dressing ingredients.

In a bowl, combine the baby spinach, pineapple, mango, tomatoes, kiwi berries, red onion, jalapeños and half of the cilantro. Pour on half the salad dressing and toss.

Top with the cooked shrimp and sprinkle with the remaining cilantro.

Serve with the remaining dressing, lime wedges and tortilla chips.

1 tbsp (15 ml) vegetable oil

8 oz (227 g) raw shrimp, peeled and deveined, tails removed

2 cloves garlic, peeled and minced

¼ tsp salt

¼ tsp freshly ground black pepper

½ tsp paprika

¼ tsp red pepper flakes

1 cup (30 g) packed baby spinach leaves

1 small pineapple, peeled and chopped into small chunks

1 large ripe mango, peeled, pitted and chopped into small chunks

10 grape tomatoes, quartered

10 kiwi berries, sliced in half, or 1 kiwifruit, peeled and chopped into small chunks

½ red onion, finely chopped

2 jalapeño peppers, sliced

⅓ cup (13 g) chopped fresh cilantro, divided

LIME DRESSING

Juice of 2 limes

3 tbsp (45 ml) extra virgin olive oil

1 tbsp (20 g) honey

¼ tsp salt

¼ tsp freshly ground black pepper

¼ tsp red pepper flakes

2 tbsp (5 g) finely chopped cilantro

TO SERVE

Lime wedges

Tortilla chips

SHRIMP PRIMAVERA PASTA SALAD

Tender yet still crisp vegetables tossed together with pasta and shrimp and served with a black pepper and lemon dressing. I love this one for dinner, but any leftovers can be eaten for lunch straight from the refrigerator.

I buy ready-cooked shrimp for this dish as a time saver, but you can cook the shrimp in the skillet with the vegetables, if you prefer.

SERVES 4

In a small bowl, stir together all the dressing ingredients.

In a bowl, combine the shrimp and cooked pasta and add 2 tablespoons (30 ml) of the dressing. Stir and cover. Let marinate at room temperature while you cook the vegetables.

In a large skillet, heat the oil over medium-high heat. Add the zucchini, broccoli and asparagus and cook for 5 minutes, stirring often.

Add the snap peas, garlic, salt and pepper and cook for an additional 2 to 3 minutes, or until the vegetables have started to soften yet still retain some crunch.

Add the tomatoes and cook for 1 minute, to soften slightly. Turn off the heat and allow to cool for 5 minutes, then stir in the spinach. The residual heat will wilt the spinach slightly.

Add the shrimp mixture to the pan and toss everything together, then transfer to a serving bowl.

Serve with the remaining dressing and a sprinkling of Parmesan.

TIP: Run the pasta under cold water after cooking, to prevent it from sticking together.

BLACK PEPPER AND LEMON DRESSING

Juice of 1 lemon

3 tbsp (45 ml) olive oil

¼ tsp salt

½ tsp freshly ground black pepper

1 clove garlic, peeled and minced

½ tsp light brown sugar

1 tbsp (4 g) finely chopped fresh parsley

SHRIMP SALAD

8 oz (227 g) cooked medium shrimp, peeled, deveined, tails removed

3 cups (450 g) cooked and cooled penne pasta (see Tip)

2 tbsp (30 ml) olive oil

1 zucchini, sliced into bite-size chunks

1 head broccoli, broken in florets

4 oz (113 g) asparagus, ends trimmed

1 cup (85 g) snap peas

2 cloves garlic, peeled and minced

½ tsp salt

½ tsp freshly ground black pepper

10 mixed-color tomatoes, sliced in half

3 cups (90 g) packed baby spinach leaves

3 tbsp (15 g) shredded Parmesan cheese

COCONUT SHRIMP SALAD WITH ASIAN SLAW

My husband, Chris, made me coconut shrimp just after we moved into our first apartment about fifteen years ago. The kitchen was a tiny 3-foot (90-cm)-square area in the corner of the living space. You could literally touch every surface at the same time!

The shrimp was so delicious, I had to get the recipe out of him. It's a great addition to a homemade Chinese banquet, but I also like to serve it for a weekend lunch with crispy Asian slaw and sriracha dressing.

SERVES 4

In a skillet, heat ¼ cup (60 ml) of the oil over medium-high heat.

Meanwhile, pat the shrimp with paper towels to ensure they're not too damp.

Take 3 bowls. Add the flour, salt and black pepper to the first bowl; mix the egg and coconut milk in the second bowl; and mix the panko and coconut in the third bowl.

Coat the shrimp in the flour, then dip into the egg mixture and finally, coat in the coconut mixture.

When the oil is hot—you can tell it's hot enough by tossing in a couple of the panko bread crumbs; if they sizzle and start to brown very quickly, it's ready—add in the shrimp. Cook on 1 side until golden brown, about 2 minutes, then turn over and cook the other side until golden brown, 1 to 2 minutes.

Remove from the skillet and transfer to a bowl lined with paper towels to remove any excess oil.

In a small bowl, stir together all the dressing ingredients.

In a large serving bowl, arrange the cabbage, onion, scallions, carrots, bell peppers and ¾ cup (30 g) of the cilantro. Drizzle with a little of the dressing.

Add the coconut shrimp and top with the remaining cilantro, sesame seeds and red pepper flakes.

Serve with the rest of the salad dressing.

COCONUT SHRIMP

¼ cup (60 ml) vegetable oil

8 oz (227 g) raw shrimp, peeled, deveined, tails removed

3 tbsp (23 g) all-purpose flour

Good pinch of salt and pepper

1 large egg

⅓ cup (80 ml) canned coconut milk

5 tbsp (35 g) panko bread crumbs

¼ cup (21 g) unsweetened shredded coconut

SRIRACHA DRESSING

2 tbsp (30 ml) olive oil

1 tbsp (15 ml) sriracha

1 small clove garlic, peeled and minced

1½ tbsp (30 g) honey

Juice of ½ lime

Pinch of salt and pepper

ASIAN SLAW

1 sweetheart cabbage, finely sliced

½ red onion, thinly sliced

3 scallions, sliced into thin strips

2 carrots, peeled and sliced into thin strips

1 red bell pepper, thinly sliced

1 yellow bell pepper, thinly sliced

1 green bell pepper, thinly sliced

1 cup (40 g) chopped fresh cilantro, divided

1 tsp sesame seeds

½ tsp red pepper flakes

MUST-TRY CHEESE AND EGG SALADS

If someone says "cheese salad" to me, I immediately think ploughman's. If they say "egg salad," my mind goes straight to tuna niçoise.

It's easy to get stuck in that same way of thinking, but I want to show you how cheese- and egg-based salads can be so much more.

If you're looking for inspiration minus the meat (we'll ignore the bacon bits in the grilled zucchini salad [page 112] for the moment—although bacon bits are very hard to ignore), simply start with what you enjoy.

Think of your main flavor, and work from there.

Love fried eggs for breakfast? Let's add piles of little gem lettuce, slices of juicy figs, plus some toasted croutons to dip into that runny egg yolk (page 107)!

Daydreaming about eating that simple-but-amazing crispy *saganaki* in a backstreet cafe in Rhodes? Let's re-create in salad format with juicy fresh tomatoes in a rainbow of colors (Saganaki Salad with Mixed Tomatoes, page 100).

All these recipes are a meal in their own right, but some could also be served as an appetizer, side dish or even as party food.

Brie-stuffed mushrooms on a bed of arugula (page 116) always go first on the Christmas party table, and the Burrata Salad Platter (page 119) makes an impressive crowd-pleaser.

These cheese and egg salad recipes are inspired partly by travels and partly by my favorite cuisines.

CRISPY HALLOUMI CUBES WITH RED GRAPEFRUIT AND POMEGRANATE DRIZZLE

A light and tasty salad with peppery arugula, zingy grapefruit and pomegranate to cut the saltiness of the halloumi. If you prefer not to coat the halloumi, you can simply fry it in a lightly oiled skillet or grill pan and serve with the rest of the salad. Perfect for a weekend summer lunch.

SERVES 4

Slice the halloumi into ½-inch (1.3-cm) cubes. Sprinkle with the flour, white pepper and smoked paprika, then toss together to coat.

In a large skillet, heat the oil over medium-high heat. Add the halloumi cubes and cook, turning, until golden on all sides, 3 to 4 minutes. Remove from the oil and transfer to a plate lined with paper towels to remove any excess oil.

To prepare the pomegranate drizzle, in a small pitcher, stir together all the drizzle ingredients.

Arrange the arugula and baby spinach leaves on 4 plates. Slice the cucumber in half lengthwise and scoop out the seeds with a teaspoon. Slice the cucumber into thin slices and arrange on top of the salad leaves.

Divide the grapefruit segments and halloumi among the plates and sprinkle with the pine nuts, pumpkin seeds, flaked almonds and pomegranate arils.

Drizzle with the pomegranate drizzle before serving.

HALLOUMI

1 (8-oz [227-g]) block halloumi cheese

½ cup (60 g) all-purpose flour

Pinch of ground white pepper

½ tsp smoked paprika

3 tbsp (45 ml) olive oil

POMEGRANATE DRIZZLE

¼ cup (60 ml) pomegranate juice

¼ cup (60 ml) olive oil

1 tsp honey

1 tbsp (15 ml) balsamic vinegar

Pinch of salt

Pinch of freshly ground black pepper

SALAD

3 cups (90 g) packed mixed arugula and baby spinach leaves

1 small cucumber

2 Ruby Red grapefruits, skin removed with a knife, flesh sliced into segments

3 tbsp (27 g) pine nuts

2 tbsp (18 g) pumpkin seeds

2 tbsp (14 g) flaked almonds, toasted

Arils of ½ pomegranate (see Tips on page 125)

GRILLED ROMAINE WITH MANCHEGO, WALNUTS AND DATES

Grilled lettuce may sound a little bizarre, but a crispy flavorful lettuce, such as romaine, tastes amazing when brushed with a little balsamic vinegar and oil and then grilled until lightly charred. If you want to make this vegetarian, you can swap out the Manchego cheese for a sharp vegetarian cheddar or a vegetarian Italian-style hard cheese.

SERVES 4

In a small bowl, stir together all the dressing ingredients.

Heat a cast-iron grill pan over high heat until hot.

Slice the romaine hearts in half lengthwise, and brush the cut sides with the dressing. Place the romaine, cut side down, on the hot pan and cook on 1 side only, for 2 to 3 minutes, or until lightly charred.

Remove the romaine from the pan and transfer, cut side up, to a serving plate.

Top with the dates and walnuts. Arrange the sliced pears on the plates and scatter with the Manchego cheese. Serve with the remaining dressing.

BALSAMIC DRESSING

¼ cup (60 ml) good-quality balsamic vinegar

6 tbsp (90 ml) olive oil

½ tsp salt

½ tsp freshly ground black pepper

SALAD

4 romaine lettuce hearts

8 Medjool dates, pitted and cut into small chunks

½ cup (64 g) roughly chopped walnuts

2 pears, cored and thinly sliced

3 oz (85 g) Manchego cheese, shaved into thin strips, using a vegetable peeler

HALLOUMI AND GRILLED BROCCOLI SALAD

I love that good old squeaky cheese, especially when grilled until lovely and golden. Since we're using the grill pan anyway, I like to add some tender-stemmed broccoli and fine asparagus.

Plate with slices of juicy ripe fruit. I'm using peaches and figs, but dried fruit, such as cranberries, dates and apricots, also works really well with this salad.

SERVES 4

Heat a cast-iron grill pan over high heat and brush with the oil. Place the halloumi slices on the pan and cook for 2 to 3 minutes each side, or until grill lines appear. Remove from the pan.

In a small bowl, stir together the tablespoon (15 ml) of oil, salt and black pepper. Brush the broccoli, asparagus and potato slices with the oil and place on the pan. Cook, turning a couple of times, for 2 to 3 minutes, or until grill marks appear. Remove from the pan.

Meanwhile, prepare the lemon chili pesto. In a small bowl, mix together the basil pesto, lemon zest, half of the lemon juice and the red pepper flakes. Taste and add more lemon juice, if required.

On a large salad platter, arrange the salad leaves. Top with the halloumi, broccoli, asparagus, potatoes, sun-dried tomatoes, pine nuts and lemon zest. Spoon dollops of the pesto on top.

1 tbsp (15 ml) olive oil, plus more for brushing

8 oz (227 g) halloumi, sliced

¼ tsp salt

¼ tsp freshly ground black pepper

4 oz (113 g) tender-stemmed broccoli, ends trimmed

15 to 20 slim asparagus stalks

8 cooked baby new potatoes, skin on, sliced

3 cups (90 g) packed mixed salad leaves

½ cup (55 g) oil-packed sun-dried tomatoes

1 tbsp (9 g) pine nuts

Zest of 1 lemon

LEMON CHILI PESTO
½ cup (120 ml) fresh basil pesto

Zest and juice of 1 lemon, divided

½ tsp red pepper flakes

HASSELBACK HONEY CARROT SALAD WITH CHICKPEAS AND FETA

I love how pretty these Hasselback carrots are. They're cooked in the oven until sweet and tender, then topped with smoky chickpeas and creamy feta. If you like spicy food, try sprinkling a good pinch of chili powder onto the carrots with the salt and pepper. It gives them a real kick!

SERVES 4

Preheat the oven to 375°F (191°C). Line a baking sheet with a silicone liner. This will prevent the delicate carrots from sticking to the pan.

Place a carrot on a cutting board. Place a chopstick along either side of the carrot, then make cuts, widthwise, all the way down the carrot. The chopsticks are to prevent your knife going all the way through and cutting the carrot in half, so make sure you don't use your best chopsticks as they may get a little scratched!

Repeat with the rest of the carrots, and carefully place the carrots in a single layer on the prepared baking sheet.

Brush the carrots with 1 tablespoon (15 ml) of the olive oil, then sprinkle with the salt and pepper and drizzle with the honey.

Bake for 25 to 30 minutes, or until the carrots are lightly browned and tender.

Meanwhile, in a small skillet, heat the remaining tablespoon (15 ml) of olive oil. Add the drained chickpeas and smoked paprika. Cook, stirring often, for 5 minutes, or until the chickpeas are slightly crispy.

Arrange the watercress and radicchio on 4 plates and drizzle with the extra virgin olive oil. Sprinkle with a pinch of salt and pepper, if you wish. Top with the Hasselback carrots and spoon the chickpeas around the carrots.

Sprinkle with the feta, flaked almonds and parsley before serving.

8 carrots, peeled

2 tbsp (30 ml) olive oil, divided

¼ tsp salt, plus a pinch more (optional)

¼ tsp freshly ground black pepper, plus a pinch more (optional)

3 tbsp (60 g) honey

1 (14-oz [397-g]) can chickpeas, drained and rinsed

2 tsp (4 g) smoked paprika

2 cups (40 g) packed watercress

1 small radicchio, finely sliced

1 tbsp (15 ml) extra virgin olive oil

½ cup (75 g) crumbled feta cheese

2 tbsp (14 g) flaked almonds, toasted

⅓ cup (20 g) chopped fresh parsley

SAGANAKI SALAD WITH MIXED TOMATOES

The best saganaki I've ever eaten was in a little backstreet café in Rhodes. It was the trip Chris and I were on when he proposed (although he proposed on the beach—not in the café). Served as a big chunk on a white plate with just a lemon wedge for garnish. Simple but amazing.

I'm sticking to the simple floured, fried and drizzled-with-lemon-juice version, but with the addition of a lovely crunchy salad with a zesty Greek dressing.

SERVES 4

Chop the tomatoes and mix in a bowl with the salt and black pepper. Set aside for 10 to 15 minutes, to release their juices.

In a small bowl, stir together all the dressing ingredients, then set aside.

In a skillet, heat the oil over medium-high heat. Dredge the kefalotyri cheese with the flour, then place in the skillet. Fry, turning once, until golden brown, 3 to 4 minutes. Turn off the heat and squeeze the lemon juice over the cheese.

Assemble the salad. On a large serving plate, arrange the tomatoes, cucumber, red onion, bell pepper and olives.

Top with the fried cheese and serve with the dressing.

TIP: Kefalotyri is the best cheese for saganaki—it's got a fairly high melting point, so it softens in the pan—especially at the edges, but it's still a little chewy and salty. You can use graviera, kefalograviera or kasseri cheese as an alternative. Use halloumi if you're really struggling to find any of those.

14 oz (397 g) mixed-color and -size tomatoes

Large pinch of salt

Large pinch of freshly ground black pepper

1 tbsp (15 ml) olive oil

7 oz (198 g) kefalotyri cheese, sliced into 1" (2.5-cm) squares (see Tip)

2 tbsp (15 g) all-purpose flour

Juice of ½ lemon

1 cucumber, peeled, seeded and sliced in half-moons

1 red onion, sliced

1 small green bell pepper, sliced widthwise and seeded

¼ cup (39 g) black kalamata olives

GREEK DRESSING

½ cup (120 ml) olive oil

2 tbsp (30 ml) red wine vinegar

Zest and juice of ½ lemon

1 clove garlic, peeled and minced

½ tsp dried oregano

Pinch of salt and pepper

TURKISH EGG SALAD WITH YOGURT SAUCE AND BULGUR WHEAT

Usually a very simple—albeit stunning—breakfast dish of seasoned yogurt with poached eggs and chili butter; I wanted to serve my Turkish eggs with a few greens and grains to make it a little more filling for lunch or dinner. The bulgur wheat is mixed with fresh herbs and scallions for a lovely fresh kick—not quite a tabbouleh, but pretty close—that tastes amazing with the chili butter yogurt sauce.

SERVES 4

In a large bowl, mix together the bulgur, olive oil, cilantro, parsley, scallions, salt and pepper.

On a large serving platter, arrange the pea shoots and baby spinach. Add the bulgur mixture and top with the grape tomatoes.

Bring a large pan of water to a boil.

Prepare the yogurt sauce. In a small bowl, stir together the Greek yogurt, salt and black pepper, then spoon the seasoned yogurt onto the platter in 4 large blobs. Smooth out the yogurt into circles.

In a small skillet, heat the butter over medium heat, then stir in the garlic and red pepper flakes. Lower the heat to very low to keep the butter warm.

By now, the water should be boiling. Add the vinegar, lower the heat to a gentle simmer and give the water a stir. Carefully break the eggs, 1 at a time, into the swirling water. Cook for 3 minutes, until the white is set. Carefully remove from the pan with a slotted spoon and place 1 egg onto each circle of yogurt.

Drizzle the garlic chili butter over the eggs and sprinkle on the cilantro and a pinch of sumac.

Serve immediately with toasted flatbreads.

2 cups (364 g) cooked bulgur, warm or cold

1 tbsp (15 ml) olive oil

1 cup (40 g) packed fresh cilantro, chopped

1 cup (60 g) packed parsley, chopped

6 scallions, finely chopped

¼ tsp salt

¼ tsp freshly ground black pepper

1 cup (20 g) packed pea shoots

1 cup (30 g) packed baby spinach leaves

8 grape tomatoes, quartered

1 tsp white wine vinegar

4 large eggs

CHILI BUTTER YOGURT SAUCE

2 cups (480 g) Greek yogurt

Good pinch of salt

Good pinch of freshly ground black pepper

3 tbsp (42 g) salted butter

1 clove garlic, minced

½ tsp red pepper flakes

2 tbsp (20 g) finely chopped fresh cilantro

Pinch of sumac

TO SERVE

Toasted flatbreads

KOREAN BIBIMBAP SALAD WITH RED RICE

I think the elements of bibimbap make a fantastic salad. It's more traditionally made with cooked vegetables and warm rice mixed with raw egg yolk upon serving.

As a salad, I still like to top mine with egg, but I like a fried egg to dip all those veggies into.

Gochujang—a thick, red, fermented chili paste—is a fantastic staple to have in the refrigerator to add kick of spicy heat to meals. I find it's great as a marinade for chicken and steak, but it's a little too strong to dollop straight onto a salad. So, I'm using gochujang within a delicious dressing to drizzle on top.

SERVES 4

In a large skillet, heat the oil over medium-high heat and carefully crack the eggs into the pan. Fry for 3 to 4 minutes, or until the whites are cooked but the yolks are still runny. Remove from the pan.

Prepare the dressing. In a small bowl, whisk together all the dressing ingredients.

Divide the rice among 4 bowls. Arrange the baby spinach, carrots, radishes, scallions, bean sprouts and cucumber in the bowls.

Top each bowl with a fried egg, then sprinkle with the red pepper flakes and sesame seeds.

Drizzle with the dressing before serving.

1 tbsp (15 ml) vegetable oil

4 large eggs

1½ cups (250 g) cooked wild red rice (about ½ cup [99 g] raw), warm or cold

2 cups (60 g) packed baby spinach leaves

2 medium carrots, peeled and spiralized or sliced into thin strips

4 radishes, sliced into thin strips

4 scallions, sliced into thin strips

1 cup (100 g) packed bean sprouts (fresh is better, but from a can, drained, is fine)

1 cucumber, spiralized or sliced into thin strips

1 tsp red pepper flakes

1 tsp mixed black and white sesame seeds

GOCHUJANG DRESSING

2 tbsp (40 g) gochujang

1 tbsp (15 ml) sesame oil

2 tbsp (30 ml) olive oil

2 tbsp (30 ml) water

1 tbsp (15 ml) dark soy sauce

1 tbsp (15 ml) rice vinegar

1 tbsp (20 g) honey

FRIED EGG BREAKFAST SALAD WITH TOASTED CROUTONS

Salad for breakfast makes a great alternative to cereal or bagels. I like to warm my lettuce leaves just slightly in the pan that was used to cook the bacon. It makes such a difference to the flavor, and means the leaves don't need to be dressed with oil at the table.

SERVES 4

In a large skillet, heat 1½ teaspoons (8 ml) of the oil over high heat. Add the bacon and fry, stirring often, for 3 to 4 minutes, or until crisp.

Remove the bacon with a slotted spoon, and transfer to a bowl lined with paper towels to drain. Lower the heat to medium.

Add the lettuce leaves to the pan and let them rest there for 1 minute—just enough to warm them slightly and add a little bit of bacon flavor. Remove from the pan.

Add another 1½ teaspoons (8 ml) of the oil to the skillet and add the ciabatta cubes. Sprinkle with the salt and pepper and fry, turning often, until browned all over, about 5 minutes. Remove from the pan.

Add the remaining 1½ teaspoons (8 ml) of oil to the pan and increase the heat to medium-high. Carefully crack the eggs into the pan and fry for 3 to 4 minutes, or until the whites are cooked but the yolks are still runny. Remove from the pan.

Assemble the salad. In 4 bowls, arrange the lettuce, figs, tomatoes, bacon and fried eggs. Top each with the sliced scallions and crumbled feta and a pinch of pepper.

Drizzle with the sweet chili sauce and serve.

1½ tbsp (23 ml) vegetable oil, divided

4 strips bacon, chopped into small pieces

1 head little gem lettuce, leaves separated and washed

1 ciabatta bread, chopped into 1" (2.5-cm) cubes

¼ tsp salt

¼ tsp freshly ground black pepper, plue more to taste

4 large eggs

2 figs, sliced

8 grape tomatoes, quartered

4 scallions, sliced

2 oz (57 g) feta cheese, crumbled

2 tbsp (40 g) sweet chili sauce

GARLIC MUSHROOM AND ROASTED SQUASH SALAD

Mushrooms are one of my mum's favorite foods. I didn't like them when I was little, but I love them now. Simply sautéed in butter, seasoning and garlic, they're amazing!

They make a fantastic meat-free salad that is given a decadent feel with plenty of crumbled Gorgonzola. I'm using a selection of mushrooms for this meal, but feel free to use your favorite variety. I love to serve this salad with some thick toasted farmhouse bread to make it filling enough for dinner.

SERVES 4

Preheat the oven to 400°F (204°C). Place the butternut squash on a baking sheet and drizzle with 2 tablespoons (30 ml) of the oil. Sprinkle with ¼ teaspoon each of the salt and pepper and all of the cumin and paprika. Toss together, then place in the oven to roast for 10 minutes.

After 10 minutes, add the radishes to the squash and toss everything together again to coat the radishes in oil. Place back in the oven to roast for an additional 15 to 20 minutes, or until the butternut squash and radishes are golden.

In a skillet, combine the remaining 2 tablespoons (30 ml) of oil along with the butter. Heat over medium-high heat until the butter melts, then add the mushrooms and remaining ¼ teaspoon each of salt and pepper. Cook for 3 to 4 minutes, until the mushrooms soften, then add the garlic. Cook, stirring occasionally, for an additional 2 minutes, or until the mushrooms are lightly golden. Turn off the heat.

On 4 plates, arrange the arugula, then top with the roasted squash, radishes and garlic mushrooms.

Sprinkle the herbs over the mushrooms, then add the Gorgonzola and pine nuts before serving with slices of toasted bread.

I butternut squash (about 40 oz [1.1 kg]) peeled, seeded and chopped into bite-size chunks

¼ cup (60 ml) olive oil, divided

½ tsp salt, divided

½ tsp freshly ground black pepper, divided

¼ tsp ground cumin

¼ tsp paprika

4 radishes, quartered

2 tbsp (28 g) unsalted butter

12 oz (340 g) mixed mushrooms, such as cremini, chestnut and button, sliced

2 cloves garlic, peeled and minced

4 cups (80 g) arugula

⅓ cup (16 g) chopped fresh chives

⅓ cup (20 g) chopped fresh parsley

½ cup (55 g) crumbled Gorgonzola cheese

2 tbsp (18 g) pine nuts

Toasted bread, for serving (optional)

ROASTED MEDITERRANEAN VEGETABLES WITH HALLOUMI AND COUSCOUS

I love a good sheet pan bake, and this one is supereasy with lovely Mediterranean flavors. I cook the halloumi in the oven along with the veggies, too—saves washing an extra pan, and tastes extra-delicious with those garlic-herb juices.

Save any leftovers to serve cold for lunch with a few baby salad leaves.

SERVES 4

Preheat the oven to 400°F (204°C).

On a large baking sheet, combine the red onions, bell peppers, tomatoes, zucchini and halloumi. Lightly bash the garlic, in the skin, using a wooden spoon, and place the garlic on the pan, too.

Drizzle with the olive oil and sprinkle with the salt, black pepper and oregano. Toss it all together, using your hands, then place in the oven and roast for 25 minutes, turning everything over after 15 minutes.

In a small bowl, stir together all the dressing ingredients.

In a saucepan, combine the couscous and hot stock. Stir and bring to a boil, then cover, turn off the heat and let sit for 5 minutes. After 5 minutes, remove the lid and add the lemon zest and half of the dressing. Fluff the couscous with a fork and test for seasoning. Add an additional pinch of salt and pepper, if needed.

Separate the halloumi from the roasted vegetables. On a large serving plate, mix together the roasted vegetables with the couscous. Top with the halloumi and a sprinkling of parsley.

Drizzle with the remaining dressing before serving.

2 red onions, cut into wedges

I red bell pepper, seeded and cut into large chunks

I yellow bell pepper, seeded and cut into large chunks

6 tomatoes, sliced in half

I zucchini, chopped into rough chunks

8 oz (227 g) halloumi, sliced

4 cloves garlic, skin on

2 tbsp (30 ml) olive oil

¼ tsp salt, plus more to taste

¼ tsp freshly ground black pepper, plus more to taste

2 tsp (2 g) dried oregano

I cup (175 g) dried couscous

1²⁄₃ cups (400 ml) hot vegetable stock

Zest of I lemon

LEMON HERB DRESSING

Juice of I lemon

3 tbsp (45 ml) olive oil

¼ tsp salt

¼ tsp freshly ground black pepper

½ clove garlic, peeled and minced

½ tsp light brown sugar

2 tbsp (8 g) finely chopped fresh parsley

I tbsp (4 g) finely chopped fresh oregano, or ½ tsp dried

I tbsp (2.4 g) finely chopped fresh thyme, or ½ tsp dried

2 tbsp (8 g) finely chopped fresh parsley

GRILLED ZUCCHINI, STILTON AND PEAR SALAD WITH BACON BITS

If you've never made bacon bits before, you're missing out! I usually have to make extra, because they're eaten so quickly. Try them sprinkled on poached eggs or potato wedges.

This salad makes a fantastic dinner party starter.

I like to serve it with a light lemon dressing to cut through the saltiness of the bacon.

SERVES 4

Preheat the oven to 350°F (177°C).

Arrange the bacon slices in a single layer on a wire rack, with a baking sheet underneath to catch any drips. Bake for 25 to 30 minutes, or until the bacon is browned and crisp. Remove from the oven and allow the bacon to cool completely on the rack.

Meanwhile, prepare the dressing. In a small bowl, whisk together all the dressing ingredients.

When the bacon is cool, transfer it to a food processor and pulse for a few seconds until the bacon is broken up into crumbs.

Heat a cast-iron grill pan over high heat.

Place the zucchini ribbons in a bowl with the oil, salt and pepper. Place the zucchini ribbons on the pan and cook for 30 to 60 seconds, or until grill lines appear (no need to turn). Remove the zucchini from the pan.

On 4 plates, arrange the arugula and zucchini ribbons. Top with pear slices, crumbled Stilton, bacon bits and chopped walnuts.

Serve with the salad dressing.

8 strips bacon

2 zucchini, shaved into ribbons, using a vegetable peeler

2 tbsp (30 ml) olive oil

Good pinch of salt

Good pinch of freshly ground black pepper

3 cups (75 g) packed arugula

2 pears, cored and thinly sliced

½ cup (55 g) crumbled Stilton cheese

1 cup (128 g) roughly chopped walnuts

LEMON GARLIC DRESSING

Zest and juice of 1 lemon

1 clove garlic, peeled and minced

Good pinch of salt

Good pinch of freshly ground black pepper

3 tbsp (45 ml) olive oil

CHEDDAR, APPLE AND WALNUT SALAD

Cheddar cheese, apples, scallions and curry dressing sounds like a really strange combination, I know. But they go together so well! You just have to try it to see.

Choose sweet, tangy apples for the best salad. I love the sweet-sharp flavor of Jazz apples, but Honeycrisps are a great choice, too.

SERVES 4

In a small bowl, whisk together all the dressing ingredients.

In 4 bowls, arrange the baby salad leaves and top with cubes of cheddar.

Core and slice the apples into thin strips. Toss with the lemon juice to prevent their turning brown, then arrange on the salads.

Top each bowl with walnuts, cranberries and scallions, then drizzle with the dressing and serve.

CREAMY CURRY DRESSING

¼ cup (60 g) Greek yogurt

2 tbsp (28 g) mayonnaise

1 tbsp (3 g) finely chopped fresh chives

1 tbsp (4 g) finely chopped fresh parsley

Juice of ½ lime

1 tsp curry powder

¼ tsp salt

¼ tsp freshly ground black pepper

1 small clove garlic, peeled and crushed

2 tsp (13 g) honey

SALAD

4 cups (120 g) packed baby salad leaves

7 oz (198 g) sharp cheddar cheese, cut into small cubes

2 sweet eating apples

2 tsp (10 ml) fresh lemon juice

½ cup (64 g) roughly chopped walnuts

¼ cup (29 g) dried cranberries

8 scallions, finely sliced

BRIE-STUFFED MUSHROOM SALAD

The addition of cranberry sauce makes these mushrooms feel a little festive—so they're great for a Thanksgiving appetizer. You can replace the cranberry sauce with caramelized onions, if you'd like a more savory option.

SERVES 4

Preheat the oven to 350°F (177°C).

Remove the stems from the mushrooms—save for adding to risotto, soup or a stir-fry—and place the mushrooms, bottom up, on a baking sheet.

Place a scant teaspoon of cranberry sauce in each mushroom. Fill the mushrooms with chunks of Brie and a few thyme leaves.

Spoon the panko bread crumbs over the mushrooms and sprinkle with a good pinch each of the salt and pepper.

Drizzle the mushrooms with 2 tablespoons (30 ml) of the olive oil, then bake for 20 minutes, or until golden brown.

When the mushrooms are nearly ready, drizzle the remaining tablespoon (15 ml) of olive oil on the arugula, along with a pinch of salt and pepper, and toss to coat.

On a serving plate, arrange the baby arugula leaves and top with the sliced watermelon radish and sun-dried tomatoes.

Top with the stuffed mushrooms and sprinkle with a few fresh thyme leaves.

12 cremini mushrooms

3 tbsp (52 g) cranberry sauce

4 oz (198 g) Brie cheese, chopped into small chunks

1 tbsp (5 g) fresh thyme leaves, plus more for garnish

6 tbsp (42 g) panko bread crumbs

¼ tsp salt

½ tsp freshly ground black pepper

3 tbsp (45 ml) olive oil, divided

2 cups (50 g) packed baby arugula

1 watermelon radish, thinly sliced

½ cup (55 g) oil-packed sun-dried tomatoes

BURRATA SALAD PLATTER

I love that setting out bits and pieces from the deli counter and the refrigerator on a big wooden serving board always feels like something special. Minimal cooking; this one is mostly about arranging the ingredients.

Start with the larger items, then nestle in all the small items, so the board looks lavishly abundant and colorful. A great sharing meal when you have friends over for lunch.

SERVES 6 TO 8

Prepare the balsamic glaze. In a small saucepan, combine the balsamic vinegar, brown sugar, salt and pepper. Stir and bring to a boil, then simmer, stirring occasionally, for about 10 minutes, or until reduced by one-third. Turn off the heat and let cool, then decant into a jar. The glaze will thicken as it cools.

Prepare the platter. Heat a large cast-iron grill pan over high heat.

In a small bowl, stir together the olive oil, salt and pepper. Brush onto the asparagus.

Place the asparagus on the pan and cook, turning once, for 1 to 2 minutes, or until lightly browned. Remove from the pan.

On a large serving platter or board, arrange the burrata, asparagus and salami.

Place the tomatoes, roasted bell pepper slices, avocado, olives and pine nuts on the platter. Add the grapes, leaving the bunches intact, then arrange the cherries, apricots and dates in little piles around the rest of the platter.

Add slices of bread to the edges and tuck small bunches of basil around the platter.

Season the burrata with a pinch of salt and pepper, and drizzle with a little of the glaze.

Serve with extra glaze.

TIP: This recipe makes more of the balsamic glaze than needed. Any leftover glaze can be stored in an airtight jar in the refrigerator for 2 weeks.

BALSAMIC GLAZE

1 cup (240 ml) good-quality balsamic vinegar

¾ cup (170 g) packed light brown sugar

Pinch of salt

Pinch of freshly ground black pepper

PLATTER

1 tbsp (15 ml) olive oil

Pinch of salt

Pinch of freshly ground black pepper

4 oz (113 g) asparagus, ends trimmed

2 (4.5-oz [128-g]) balls burrata cheese, one torn into 10 to 12 pieces

6 slices Milano salami

8 slices peppered salami

10 grape tomatoes, sliced in half

4 roasted red bell peppers, from a jar, drained and sliced into strips

1 avocado, peeled, pitted and sliced

½ cup (78 g) mixed olives

¼ cup (34 g) pine nuts

Small bunch of green grapes

Small bunch of red grapes

1 cup (140 g) fresh cherries

¾ cup (98 g) dried apricots

4 Medjool dates, pitted

1 ciabatta bread, sliced

Bunch of fresh basil

Salt and freshly ground black pepper

NUTRITIOUS GRAINS, NUTS AND SEEDS

My husband would say that a salad without meat is just a side salad. He's pretty much the biggest carnivore I know, so getting him to eat and *enjoy* a salad with no meat is a testament to a bloomin' good dish.

Grains, nuts and seeds, apart from being filling and nutritious, really add something extra to a salad, so you won't even miss the meat.

These are all Chris-approved salads, with an array of flavors using inspiration from different countries and cultures. We're talking Mexican, Moroccan, Thai and Lebanese.

My favorite creamy curry dressing that made an appearance in the last chapter is back again, too, in the Chicory and Fennel Crunch Salad with Spicy Walnut Brittle (page 130)!

HERBY RED PEPPER HUMMUS SALAD WITH TOASTED PITA WEDGES

My daughter has loved hummus ever since she was tiny. Now, she packs her own lunch for school, and this superquick red pepper version is her absolute favorite. Served with a fragrant herb salad and a light lemon dressing, plus some toasted pita for dipping, it makes a fresh and tasty lunch.

SERVES 4

In a food processor, combine the bell peppers and chickpeas and blend for 1 to 2 minutes, or until smooth. Add the tahini, lemon juice, garlic, oil and salt and pepper and blend again until thick and creamy. Spoon into a bowl and sprinkle with the red pepper flakes.

In a small bowl, stir together all the dressing ingredients.

Toast the pita breads in a toaster or under a broiler until lightly browned, then slice into wedges.

Divide the hummus, in little swirls, among 4 plates. Add the baby salad leaves, parsley, chives and mint to the plates, around the hummus. Arrange the red onion, cucumber and tomato slices on the plate, then sprinkle on the mixed seeds and scallions.

Serve with the dressing and toasted pita wedges.

HUMMUS

2 roasted red bell peppers, from a jar, drained

1 (14-oz [397-g]) can chickpeas, drained and rinsed

1½ tbsp (23 g) tahini

1 tbsp (15 ml) lemon juice

1 clove garlic, peeled and minced

2 tbsp (30 ml) olive oil, plus more for drizzling

¼ tsp salt

Pinch of freshly ground black pepper

Pinch of red pepper flakes

LEMON DRESSING

Juice of 1 lemon

3 tbsp (45 ml) olive oil

¼ tsp salt

¼ tsp freshly ground black pepper

½ clove garlic, peeled and minced

½ tsp light brown sugar

To Assemble

2 pita breads

2½ cups (75 g) packed baby salad leaves

⅓ cup (20 g) chopped fresh parsley

⅓ cup (16 g) chopped fresh chives

2 sprigs fresh mint

½ red onion, thinly sliced

½ cucumber, seeded and sliced into half-moons

1 mini cucumber, sliced

3 tomatoes, sliced

¼ cup (about 35 g) mixed seeds, such as sunflower and pumpkin seeds

4 scallions, sliced into thin strips

FATTOUSH WITH SUMAC HUMMUS AND POMEGRANATE

More than a few salads in this book contain bread (carbivore over here!). It's such a good way to soak up all those delicious juices hiding under your salad leaves. This salad uses pita bread to mop up the juices from sweet, vine-ripened tomatoes.

I've also included a tip on removing the arils (seeds) from a pomegranate without leaving your kitchen looking like a crime scene!

SERVES 4

In a large, dry skillet, toast the pita breads over high heat, then tear roughly into chunks.

In a small bowl, whisk together all the dressing ingredients.

In a large bowl, combine the pita chunks, remaining salad ingredients and the dressing. Toss together and transfer to a serving dish. Allow to sit for a few minutes while you make the hummus.

To prepare the hummus, in a food processor, process the chickpeas for 1 to 2 minutes, or until smooth. Add the tahini, lemon juice, garlic, oil, all but ¼ teaspoon of the sumac, and the salt and black pepper and blend again until thick and creamy.

Spoon the hummus onto the serving dish, swirling with a spoon. Sprinkle with the red pepper flakes and remaining sumac.

TIPS: To remove the arils from the pomegranate, place the fruit on its side and slice in half, then loosen the skin slightly by pulling it outward. Over a large bowl, tuck the cut side of a pomegranate half into the palm of your hand. While cupping your hand to catch the seeds and lightly gripping the pomegranate skin with your fingers, hit the outer skin hard with a wooden spoon, until the seeds fall out into your palm. It's easier to let them fall into your hand and tip the seeds into the bowl, rather than try to let them fall directly into the bowl.

If your hands become red with pomegranate juice, wash them with water and a little baking soda or whitening toothpaste to remove the stains.

SALAD

2 pita breads

4 large vine-ripened tomatoes, chopped into bite-size chunks

½ cucumber, seeded and sliced

½ red onion, sliced

2 scallions, chopped

1 head romaine lettuce, shredded

⅓ cup (20 g) chopped fresh mint leaves

⅓ cup (20 g) chopped fresh parsley

Arils of ½ pomegranate (see Tips)

Pinch of sumac

Pinch of freshly ground black pepper

LEMON DRESSING WITH SUMAC

Juice of 1 lemon

3 tbsp (45 ml) olive oil

¼ tsp salt

¼ tsp freshly ground black pepper

½ clove garlic, peeled and minced

½ tsp light brown sugar

1 tsp sumac

SUMAC HUMMUS

1 (14-oz [397-g]) can chickpeas, drained and rinsed

1½ tbsp (23 g) tahini

1 tbsp (15 ml) fresh lemon juice

1 clove garlic, peeled and minced

2 tbsp (30 ml) olive oil, plus more for drizzling

1½ tsp (4 g) sumac, divided

¼ tsp salt

Pinch of freshly ground black pepper

Pinch of red pepper flakes

TABBOULEH WITH SMOKY EGGPLANT, FETA AND CRANBERRIES

I first came across tabbouleh a few years ago in a Lebanese restaurant, and I was blown away by the freshness and flavor. It's probably the first time I started to use parsley as an ingredient, rather than just a finishing touch. The key is to make sure you're using the freshest possible parsley with large dark green leaves.

The smoky eggplant makes a great alternative to meat, but if you want the meat, try swapping out the eggplant for sliced lamb.

SERVES 4

To prepare the tabbouleh, in a bowl, toss together all the tabbouleh ingredients. Let stand so the flavors infuse while you make the eggplant.

Heat a cast-iron grill pan or skillet over high heat. Brush the eggplant slices with olive oil on both sides, then sprinkle with the salt, garlic salt, pepper and paprika.

Place the eggplant slices on the pan and cook for 2 to 3 minutes on each side, or until browned.

Divide the tabbouleh among 4 plates. Top each with 2 eggplant slices and sprinkle with the feta, cranberries and parsley before serving.

TABBOULEH

2 cups (364 g) cooked bulgur

2 large tomatoes, chopped into small pieces

2 scallions, finely chopped

1 cup (40 g) chopped fresh cilantro

1 cup (60 g) chopped fresh parsley

2 tbsp (12 g) finely chopped fresh mint leaves

Juice of ½ lime

2 tbsp (30 ml) extra virgin olive oil

Pinch of salt

Pinch of freshly ground black pepper

SMOKY EGGPLANT

2 eggplants (about 11 oz [312 g] each), sliced into ¾" (2-cm) slices

¼ cup (60 ml) olive oil

¼ tsp salt

¼ tsp garlic salt

½ tsp freshly ground black pepper

1 tsp smoked paprika

TO ASSEMBLE

¼ cup (38 g) crumbled feta cheese

¼ cup (29 g) dried cranberries

1 tbsp (4 g) finely chopped fresh parsley

CAPRESE SORGHUM SALAD

If you've never cooked with sorghum before, it's well worth giving it a go. A great gluten-free alternative to couscous, it's packed full of nutritious goodies. It takes a bit longer to cook, but I like to make it in bulk as it can be refrigerated or frozen for future meals.

I think the delicate flavor of the sorghum works so well with the classic Caprese ingredients of tomatoes, mozzarella and basil. The arugula adds a lovely peppery touch.

SERVES 4

In a saucepan, combine the sorghum with the hot stock. Stir, bring to a boil, then cover and simmer for 45 to 50 minutes, or until the sorghum is tender. Drain off any excess liquid and fluff with a fork. Let cool to room temperature.

Meanwhile, chop the tomatoes and mix with the salt and pepper, then set aside in a bowl for 10 to 15 minutes, to release their juices.

In a small bowl, stir together all the dressing ingredients.

In a serving bowl, combine the tomatoes, including any of their juices, with the cooked sorghum and arugula. Drizzle with half of the dressing, and toss together.

Top with the mozzarella pearls and basil and serve with the remaining dressing.

1 cup (192 g) dried sorghum

3 cups (720 ml) hot vegetable stock

14 oz (397 g) mixed, vine-ripened tomatoes, at room temperature for maximum flavor

Large pinch of salt

Large pinch of freshly ground black pepper

2 cups (40 g) baby arugula

8 oz (227 g) mozzarella pearls

10 fresh basil leaves, sliced or torn

RED WINE DRESSING

¼ cup (60 ml) olive oil

2 tbsp (30 ml) red wine vinegar

1 tsp superfine sugar

1 clove garlic, peeled and minced

Pinch of salt

Pinch of freshly ground black pepper

CHICORY AND FENNEL CRUNCH SALAD WITH SPICY WALNUT BRITTLE AND CREAMY CURRY DRESSING

The inspiration for this salad comes from a trip we took to Morro Bay in California a few years ago. One of the most memorable meals was a salad with a curry dressing, fruit and spicy walnuts. I picked it off the menu because it sounded unusual, but it was so good, I was working on the curry sauce recipe the moment we got back from holiday!

SERVES 4

Line a baking sheet with a sheet of nonstick baking parchment.

Place the sugar in a small, heavy-bottomed pan and smooth with a spoon into an even layer. Place the pan over low heat. The sugar will start to melt after 5 minutes or so, starting at the edges. Don't stir; just allow the sugar to continue to melt until it's almost completely melted, about 10 minutes. Turn off the heat and let sit for an additional minute. The residual heat will allow the remaining sugar to melt.

Pour the walnuts and red pepper flakes into the sugar and, working quickly, stir everything together, then use a wooden spoon to transfer to the prepared baking sheet.

Use the back of the spoon to flatten out the mixture (be careful, it will be very hot). Then, let the brittle cool, about 10 minutes, before breaking into pieces with your hands.

In a small bowl, stir together all the dressing ingredients.

To prepare the salad, slice off the green fronds at the base of the fennel and discard. Slice the fennel in half lengthwise, then cut out the tough core at its base and discard. Cut each of the 2 fennel halves into thin slices.

On a large serving plate, arrange the fennel slices along with the endive, celery, pear, baby kale, baby salad leaves, olive oil, salt and pepper. Toss together to coat the leaves with the olive oil.

Drizzle with a little of the dressing and sprinkle with the walnut brittle. Serve with the remaining dressing.

WALNUT BRITTLE
1 cup (220 g) superfine sugar

1 cup (128 g) roughly chopped walnuts

¼ tsp red pepper flakes

CREAMY CURRY DRESSING
¼ cup (60 g) Greek yogurt

2 tbsp (28 g) mayonnaise

1 tbsp (3 g) finely chopped fresh chives

1 tbsp (4 g) finely chopped fresh parsley

Juice of ½ lime

1 tsp curry powder

Good pinch of salt

¼ tsp freshly ground black pepper

1 small clove garlic, peeled and crushed

2 tsp (13 g) honey

SALAD
1 large head fennel

1 red endive, separated into individual leaves

1 celery rib, sliced

1 sweet pear, cored and thinly sliced

1 cup (30 g) baby kale

1 cup (30 g) baby salad leaves

1 tbsp (15 ml) olive oil

Pinch of salt

Pinch of freshly ground black pepper

FALAFEL SALAD BOWL WITH POMEGRANATE AND FETA DRESSING

Falafel is a tasty chickpea-based Middle Eastern patty or ball that's fried in a little oil. It makes a fantastic alternative to meat and is so much easier to make than you might think.

This is a filling salad with spicy falafel patties and a simple creamy, tangy dressing that's perfect for dinner. You can serve the falafel hot or cold—great for lunchtime leftovers!

SERVES 4

Place all the falafel ingredients, except the oil, in a food processor and pulse until combined, but still with a little texture. Form the mixture into 12 equal patties.

In a large skillet, heat the oil over medium-high heat. Fry the falafels, turning once, until golden brown on both sides, for 5 to 6 minutes.

In a bowl, combine all the dressing ingredients and use an immersion blender or place in a small food processor, to blend until smooth.

Arrange the spinach, red onion, shredded beet, sun-dried tomatoes and cucumber slices in 4 bowls. Top each with 3 falafels. Drizzle with the dressing and sprinkle with pomegranate arils and parsley before serving.

FALAFEL

2 (14-oz [397-g]) cans chickpeas, drained and rinsed

I large red onion, chopped

2 large cloves garlic, peeled and minced

I cup (60 g) packed fresh parsley, chopped

I cup (40 g) packed fresh cilantro, chopped

Juice of ½ lemon

2 tsp (4 g) ground cumin

¾ tsp salt

½ tsp freshly ground black pepper

I tbsp (6 g) ground coriander

½ tsp red pepper flakes

2 tbsp (30 g) all-purpose flour

3 tbsp (45 ml) vegetable oil

FETA DRESSING

3 tbsp (28 g) crumbled feta cheese

3 tbsp (45 ml) heavy cream

5 tbsp (75 ml) milk

I tbsp (15 ml) olive oil

Good pinch of salt and pepper

SALAD

3 cups (90 g) packed baby spinach leaves

½ red onion, thinly sliced

I large cooked beet, peeled and shredded

½ cup (55 g) oil-packed sun-dried tomatoes

3 baby cucumbers or ¼ regular cucumber, thinly sliced

Arils of ½ pomegranate (see Tips on page 125)

I tbsp (4 g) finely chopped fresh parsley

SMOKY CAULIFLOWER SALAD WITH COUSCOUS AND SRIRACHA MAYO

Boiled cauliflower on its own can be boring, but it's actually quite a versatile vegetable. It can take strong flavors, such as garlic and chiles, without losing its personality. Use it for cauliflower gratin, turn it into cauliflower rice or you could even cut it into "steaks." I like it chopped into florets and browned in the oven with a good drizzle of sriracha mayo. Serve with couscous salad for a filling meat-free dinner.

SERVES 4

Preheat the oven to 400°F (204°C).

Place the cauliflower florets on a large baking sheet and drizzle with the oil. Sprinkle with the salt, garlic salt, black pepper and smoked paprika. Toss everything together and bake for 20 minutes, or until the cauliflower is golden and tender.

Meanwhile, prepare the couscous salad. In a large saucepan, heat the oil over medium heat. Add the onion and cook, stirring often, for 5 minutes, or until the onion softens. Add the garlic, salt, black pepper, cumin, paprika and celery salt and stir together. Cook for an additional 2 minutes, or until the spices release their fragrance.

Add the couscous and hot stock. Stir and bring to a boil, then cover, turn off the heat and let sit for 5 minutes.

After 5 minutes, remove the lid and fluff the couscous with a fork. Add the red and green bell peppers, tomatoes, scallions and parsley to the couscous and toss together.

Transfer to a large serving plate and top with the roasted cauliflower.

In a small bowl, stir together the mayonnaise and sriracha and drizzle on top of the cauliflower before serving.

SMOKY CAULIFLOWER

1 large head cauliflower, broken into florets

2 tbsp (30 ml) olive oil

¼ tsp salt

¼ tsp garlic salt

¼ tsp black pepper

1½ tsp (4 g) smoked paprika

COUSCOUS SALAD

1 tbsp (15 ml) olive oil

1 onion, finely chopped

2 cloves garlic, peeled and minced

½ tsp salt

½ tsp freshly ground black pepper

1 tsp ground cumin

½ tsp paprika

½ tsp celery salt

1 cup (175 g) dried couscous

1⅔ cups (400 ml) hot vegetable stock

1 red bell pepper, seeded and finely chopped

1 green bell pepper, seeded and finely chopped

10 grape tomatoes, quartered

5 scallions, chopped

1 cup (60 g) chopped fresh parsley

SRIRACHA MAYO

¼ cup (60 g) mayonnaise

2 tbsp (30 ml) sriracha

ROASTED SQUASH SALAD WITH CARAMELIZED FIGS

Regular butternut squash is a great staple to have in the vegetable drawer, but when it starts to get colder, I get so excited to see all the other squash varieties in the shops: onion squash with its rough-looking, slightly wrinkly skin . . . kabocha squash, small and seemingly full of seeds, but amazing roasted and stuffed . . . acorn squash with its bumps and ridges. You can use any squash you like for this salad, but I like to use a dark-skinned, drier squash for a sweeter, nuttier taste. Acorn and kabocha are great options, but I'm using Crown Prince, which is a larger squash with vibrantly sweet orange flesh. It's bigger than acorn or kabocha, but still really tasty. One Crown Prince squash will be enough for this salad plus leftovers for soup.

SERVES 4

Preheat the oven to 375°F (191°C).

Without removing its skin, cut the squash into 1-inch (2.5-cm) slices, remove and discard the seeds, then cut each slice into half-moons.

Place on a baking sheet along with the golden and striped beets. Add the olive oil, salt, pepper, cumin and paprika. Toss together to coat. Smooth to a single layer and roast in the oven for 15 minutes.

Turn over the squash. Dust the figs with the brown sugar and add to the baking sheet. Roast for an additional 10 minutes, or until the squash is tender and the figs are caramelized.

Meanwhile, prepare the dressing. In a small bowl, stir together all the dressing ingredients.

Divide the baby spinach among 4 plates. Top with the squash, beets and figs, then sprinkle with the feta cheese, pomegranate arils and pecans.

Serve with the dressing.

1 Crown Prince squash, skin on, cut into thick slices and seeded

1 golden or red beet, peeled and sliced into wedges

1 striped or red beet, peeled and sliced into wedges

2 tbsp (30 ml) olive oil

¼ tsp salt

¼ tsp freshly ground black pepper

¼ tsp ground cumin

½ tsp paprika

4 fresh figs, sliced in half

1 tbsp (9 g) light brown sugar

2 cups (60 g) packed baby spinach leaves

½ cup (55 g) crumbled feta cheese

¼ cup (56 g) pomegranate arils (see Tips, page 125)

¼ cup (28 g) pecans, roughly chopped

RED WINE DRESSING

¼ cup (60 ml) olive oil

2 tbsp (30 ml) red wine vinegar

1 tsp superfine sugar

1 clove garlic, peeled and minced

Pinch of salt

Pinch of freshly ground black pepper

THAI-STYLE SLAW WITH PEANUT DRESSING

Full of color and crunch and flavor, this Thai-style slaw makes a great side dish to go with grilled chicken or steak. Alternatively, serve it on its own for a light lunch. If you like your slaw spicier, you can add some freshly chopped chiles to the veggies, or an extra squirt of sriracha to the dressing (or both!).

SERVES 4

In a large bowl, combine all the slaw ingredients.

For the dressing, in a small bowl, whisk together all the dressing ingredients, using a small whisk or fork. Whisk until the peanut butter is blended into the dressing.

Pour the dressing over the slaw mixture and toss together.

Sprinkle with the peanuts and crunchy onions, then serve.

SLAW

1 sweetheart cabbage, finely sliced (about 17 oz [482 g] sliced)

½ red cabbage, finely sliced (about 22 oz [624 g] sliced)

3 tbsp (8 g) chopped fresh cilantro

½ red onion, thinly sliced

2 scallions, sliced into thin strips

2 carrots, peeled and sliced into thin strips

1 red bell pepper, seeded and thinly sliced

1 yellow bell pepper, seeded and thinly sliced

THAI PEANUT DRESSING

1 tbsp (16 g) smooth peanut butter

2 tbsp (30 ml) dark soy sauce

1 tbsp (15 ml) olive oil

1 tbsp (15 ml) sriracha

¼ tsp minced fresh ginger

1 small clove garlic, peeled and minced

1 tbsp (20 g) honey

Juice of ½ lime

TO SERVE

¼ cup (36 g) chopped roasted peanuts

2 tbsp (26 g) crunchy fried onions (available ready-made)

QUINOA AND KALE SALAD WITH ROASTED SQUASH, PLUMS AND GOAT CHEESE

It took me a while to jump on the quinoa bandwagon. I thought it sounded like one of those boring, tasteless superfoods that was good for you but provided no pleasure whatsoever.

I was so wrong. Cooked in stock, it's got a light nutty flavor with a nice bite to it. I love to mix it together with roasted vegetables—I've just used squash in this recipe, but sweet potato, zucchini, peppers, onions, broccoli, etc., all work really well—and a pile of fresh herbs. Finished with some creamy goat cheese and sliced plums, this is a really moreish lunch.

SERVES 4

Preheat the oven to 375°F (191°C). Place the cubes of squash on a baking sheet and drizzle with the olive oil. Sprinkle with the salt and pepper and toss everything together. Roast in the oven for 20 to 25 minutes, or until tender.

Meanwhile, in a saucepan, combine the quinoa and the stock. Bring to a boil, then cover, lower the heat to medium and simmer for 20 minutes. Then, fluff with a fork.

In a small bowl, whisk together all the vinaigrette ingredients.

Assemble the salad in a large bowl. Combine the warm quinoa, roasted squash, plums, cavolo nero, goat cheese and chopped herbs.

Toss everything together, then drizzle with the vinaigrette and serve.

1 butternut squash (about 40 oz [1.1 kg]), peeled, seeded and chopped into 1" (2.5-cm) cubes

2 tbsp (30 ml) olive oil

¼ tsp salt

¼ tsp freshly ground black pepper

1 cup (180 g) dried quinoa

2¼ cups (540 ml) vegetable stock

6 small plums, sliced in half and pitted

2 cups (60 g) packed shredded cavolo nero (lacinato kale) or regular kale

4.5 oz (128 g) soft goat cheese, chopped into bite-size chunks

1 cup (60 g) packed mixed herbs, such as cilantro, parsley and mint, chopped

CILANTRO LIME VINAIGRETTE

2 tbsp (30 ml) fresh lime juice

1 tsp white wine vinegar

½ clove garlic, minced

1 tbsp (20 g) honey

Pinch of salt

3 tbsp (45 ml) extra virgin olive oil

⅓ cup (10 g) chopped fresh cilantro

MOROCCAN COUSCOUS SALAD WITH ORANGE AND APRICOT

A fragrant, filling and colorful salad that makes a fantastic packed lunch. This salad is a meal in itself, but you can also serve it as a side dish. It works great with harissa-spiced chicken or lamb.

SERVES 4

In a large saucepan, heat the oil over medium heat. Add the onion and cook, stirring often, for 5 minutes, or until the onion softens.

Add the chickpeas, garlic, salt, black pepper, cumin, paprika and celery salt and stir together. Cook for an additional 5 minutes, or until the spices release their fragrance and the chickpeas have warmed through.

Add the couscous and hot stock. Stir and bring to a boil, then cover, turn off the heat and let sit for 5 minutes.

Meanwhile, use a sharp knife to cut the skin from the oranges. Over a bowl, cut the oranges into segments, reserving any juice the bowl catches.

Take the lid off the saucepan and add the reserved orange juice to the couscous, then fluff up using a fork.

Add the orange segments, red and green bell peppers, tomatoes, spinach, apricots, scallions, ½ cup (30 g) of the parsley and half of the pomegranate arils. Toss together and transfer to a serving bowl.

Top with the remaining ½ cup (30 g) of parsley and pomegranate arils before serving.

1 tbsp (15 ml) vegetable oil

1 onion, finely chopped

1 (14-oz [397-g]) can chickpeas, drained and rinsed

2 cloves garlic, peeled and minced

½ tsp salt

½ tsp freshly ground black pepper

1 tsp ground cumin

½ tsp paprika

½ tsp celery salt

1 cup (175 g) dried couscous

1⅔ cups (400 ml) hot vegetable stock

2 oranges

1 red bell pepper, seeded and finely chopped

1 green bell pepper, seeded and finely chopped

2 large tomatoes, diced

2 cups (60 g) packed baby spinach leaves

¾ cup (98 g) dried apricots, roughly chopped

2 scallions, sliced into thin strips

1 cup (60 g) packed fresh parsley, chopped, divided

Arils of ½ pomegranate, divided (see Tips on page 125)

MEDITERRANEAN LENTIL SALAD

Possibly the easiest salad in the book, this one uses canned lentils mixed with fresh Mediterranean-style vegetables and feta cheese. Great as a main dish for lunch, or as a side dish to go with grilled chicken or fish for dinner.

I make a double batch of this for ready-to-eat make-ahead lunches during the week.

SERVES 4

In a bowl, combine all the salad ingredients and toss together.

In a small pitcher, stir all the dressing ingredients together, then drizzle half over the lentil salad.

Serve the rest of the dressing with the lentil salad.

SALAD

2 cups (400 g) cooked or canned lentils, drained and rinsed

2 baby cucumbers, sliced

8 grape tomatoes, quartered

1 small red onion, thinly sliced

3 baby bell peppers (mixed colors), seeded and sliced

½ cup (75 g) crumbled feta cheese

⅓ cup (20 g) chopped fresh parsley

GREEK DRESSING

½ cup (120 ml) olive oil

2 tbsp (30 ml) red wine vinegar

Zest and juice of ½ lemon

1 clove garlic, peeled and minced

½ tsp dried oregano

Pinch of salt

Pinch of freshly ground black pepper

LOADED STREET CORN SALAD
WITH MANCHEGO

Sweet, juicy corn, tossed together with crunchy onions and jalapeños, then finished with piles of aromatic cilantro and creamy Manchego cheese.

I could eat the whole bowl of this stuff in front of the TV in my PJ's . . .

If you did want to share, it makes a great side dish for chicken or fish. You can also cook the corn under the broiler or on the barbecue, if you prefer.

SERVES 4

Heat a cast-iron grill pan over medium to high heat and brush with the oil. When hot, place the ears of corn on the pan and cook, turning regularly, for 7 to 10 minutes, or until lightly charred.

Remove from the heat and let cool for 5 minutes, then carefully slice off the corn kernels, using a sharp knife.

Transfer the corn to a large serving bowl and stir in the butter, garlic salt, black pepper, paprika and red pepper flakes. Add in the jalapeño, red onion, parsley, half of the cilantro, ¼ cup (25 g) of the cheese and the lime juice.

Toss together, then sprinkle the remaining Manchego and cilantro on top.

1 tbsp (15 ml) vegetable oil

4 ears of corn

2 tbsp (28 g) salted butter, at room temperature

½ tsp garlic salt

½ tsp freshly ground black pepper

1 tsp smoked paprika

1 tsp red pepper flakes

1 jalapeño pepper, finely chopped

½ red onion, finely chopped

2 tbsp (8 g) finely chopped fresh parsley

⅓ cup (13 g) chopped fresh cilantro, divided

½ cup (50 g) finely grated Manchego cheese, divided

1 tbsp (15 ml) lime juice

POTATOES, PASTA, RICE AND BREAD FOR ANY OCCASION

I'm a carb girl. I'm pretty sure I could think of a different way of serving potatoes every meal for a week.

The thing about carbs is they're filling, and great for an energy hit. On their own, they can be a little boring, but often a couple of simple ingredients can turn them into something special.

Dry toast = yuck. Toast with salted French butter? = The best.

How about garlic butter toast croutons with fragrant basil, juicy vine-ripened tomatoes and creamy mozzarella (check out Garlic Crouton Salad with Basil and Mozzarella on page 161)—so good!

These are my "I can't resist loads of carbs, but I want to feel energized, not sleepy" salads.

RAINBOW NOODLE SALAD WITH THAI PEANUT DRESSING

A crunchy, zingy vegetarian salad with my supereasy Thai-style peanut dressing. Use a mandoline, if you have one, to slice the vegetables—it will make the chopping process *so* much quicker.

If you wanted to add meat to this salad, grilled chicken or steak work really well.

SERVES 4

Cook the noodles per the pack instructions, then drain and rinse with cold water and toss with the sesame oil to prevent them from sticking together.

Use a mandoline to julienne the red cabbage, carrot, radishes, yellow and red bell peppers and green cabbage, or slice finely if you don't have a mandoline. Finely slice the scallions into 1-inch (2.5-cm)-long strips.

Prepare the dressing. In a small bowl, whisk together all the dressing ingredients, using a small whisk or fork, until the peanut butter is well incorporated.

Assemble the salad. In a large bowl combine the vegetables and noodles, then toss together to mix. Drizzle with the dressing

To serve, divide among 4 bowls and top with the cilantro, sesame seeds and chopped peanuts.

7 oz (198 g) dried, thin egg noodles

1 tsp toasted sesame oil

¼ (11-oz [312-g]) red cabbage

1 large carrot, peeled

4 radishes

1 yellow bell pepper

1 red bell pepper

½ (8.5-oz [241-g]) green sweetheart cabbage

5 scallions

THAI PEANUT DRESSING

1 tbsp (16 g) smooth peanut butter

2 tbsp (30 ml) dark soy sauce

1 tbsp (15 ml) olive oil

1 tbsp (15 ml) sriracha

¼ tsp minced fresh ginger

1 small clove garlic, peeled and minced

1 tbsp (20 g) honey

Juice of ½ lime

TO SERVE

Handful of fresh cilantro, roughly torn

1 tbsp (8 g) sesame seeds

2 tbsp (18 g) chopped, unsalted peanuts

PASTA SALAD WITH GRILLED CHICKEN

A great way to use up leftover pasta or chicken. My whole family loves this salad. It's quick, simple and tasty—checking all the dinner boxes!

I like to serve it with a creamy Parmesan ranch dressing, but it also goes really well with a little balsamic and olive oil, if you don't want a creamy version.

SERVES 4

Bring a large saucepan of water to a boil and add the pasta. Cook for 12 minutes, or until al dente, then drain and rinse in cold water to prevent the pasta from sticking together.

Place the 2 chicken breasts in a large resealable plastic bag and flatten them, using a rolling pin. Remove from the bag and drizzle the chicken with the oil, then sprinkle with the salt and pepper.

Heat a cast-iron grill pan over high heat and brush with oil, then add the 2 chicken breasts. Cook for 4 to 5 minutes on each side, or until the chicken is lightly browned and no longer pink in the middle.

Meanwhile, prepare the dressing. In a small bowl, stir together all the dressing ingredients until fully combined.

Once cooked, transfer the chicken to a cutting board and slice into strips.

In a serving bowl, combine the pasta, chicken, pea shoots, arugula, cucumber, tomatoes and red onion and toss together.

Drizzle with the salad dressing and serve.

10 oz (283 g) dried bowtie pasta

2 chicken breasts

1 tbsp (15 ml) vegetable oil, plus more for the pan

¼ tsp salt

¼ tsp freshly ground black pepper

1 cup (20 g) packed pea shoots

1 cup (25 g) packed arugula

½ cucumber, chopped into small chunks

10 grape tomatoes, quartered

½ red onion, thinly sliced

PARMESAN RANCH DRESSING

¼ cup (60 g) mayonnaise

¼ cup (60 g) sour cream

1 clove garlic, peeled and minced

1 tsp fresh lemon juice

½ tsp English mustard powder

¼ tsp onion powder

½ cup (40 g) shredded Parmesan cheese

1 tbsp (4 g) fresh dill, chopped

1 tbsp (3 g) fresh chives, chopped

Pinch of salt

Pinch of freshly ground black pepper

WINTER NOODLE SALAD WITH MISO DRESSING

Even though this is a cold salad, the miso dressing with red pepper flakes and ginger make it feel comforting and satisfying.

If you would like to serve it warm, don't run the noodles and broccoli under cold water. Just toss with sesame oil as soon as they're cooked, then mix with the cold veggies.

You can also warm the miso dressing in a saucepan for a few minutes before pouring onto the salad.

SERVES 4

Bring a saucepan of water to a boil and add the egg noodles and broccoli. Simmer for 3 to 4 minutes, or until the noodles are cooked and the broccoli is warmed through, but still has a bit of crunch.

Drain and run under cold water to stop the cooking process, then toss with the sesame oil to prevent the noodles from sticking together.

Prepare the dressing. In a small bowl, whisk together all the dressing ingredients until fully combined.

In a large bowl, combine the noodles, broccoli, cabbage, carrots, bell pepper, cucumber and cilantro and toss together with half of the dressing.

Sprinkle the sesame seeds on top and serve with the remaining dressing.

8 oz (227 g) dried thin egg noodles

4 oz (113 g) tender-stemmed broccoli, ends trimmed

1 tbsp (15 ml) sesame oil

1 head tender-leafed green cabbage, sliced into thin strips (about 10 oz [284 g] sliced)

2 medium carrots, peeled and spiralized

1 red bell pepper, seeded and sliced

1 small cucumber, spiralized

⅓ cup (13 g) chopped fresh cilantro

1 tsp mixed black and white sesame seeds

MISO DRESSING

2 tbsp (32 g) white miso paste

2 tbsp (30 ml) olive oil

1 tbsp (15 ml) rice vinegar

1 tbsp (15 ml) fresh lemon juice

2 tbsp (40 g) honey

1 clove garlic, peeled and minced

1 tsp minced fresh ginger

¼ tsp freshly ground black pepper

½ tsp red pepper flakes

ORZO PASTA SALAD WITH SALMON

A filling and nutritious salad, served warm—making it great for a winter dinner. The salmon and veggies are all cooked in one pan with slightly spicy seasoned oil that is then used as the salad dressing at the end.

Any leftovers can be kept, covered, in the refrigerator and served cold for lunch the next day.

SERVES 4

Preheat the oven to 375°F (191°C).

On a large baking sheet, arrange the salmon fillets, sweet potatoes, zucchini and red onion in a single layer.

In a small bowl, stir together the olive oil, salt, black pepper, garlic, red pepper flakes, brown sugar, paprika and cumin and drizzle it all over the salmon and vegetables on the pan.

Bake the salmon and vegetables for 10 minutes, then add the asparagus and green beans to the pan. Brush with oil from the pan and bake for an additional 10 minutes, or until the salmon is cooked through and the vegetables are tender, checking the oven after 5 minutes, and remove anything that starts to look too brown, if required.

Meanwhile, in a saucepan, combine the orzo with the hot stock and bring to a boil. Simmer for 7 minutes, then drain.

Remove the cooked salmon from the pan and flake with a fork. Place in a large serving bowl along with the roasted vegetables and any oil that's left on the pan. Add the cooked orzo, baby spinach, grape tomatoes and the lemon zest and juice and toss together.

Sprinkle with the parsley and serve.

2 salmon fillets

2 medium sweet potatoes, peeled and chopped into 1" (2.5-cm) cubes

1 large zucchini, chopped into 1" (2.5-cm) cubes

1 red onion, sliced into wedges

3 tbsp (45 ml) olive oil

½ tsp salt

½ tsp freshly ground black pepper

3 cloves garlic, peeled and minced

½ tsp red pepper flakes

1 tbsp (9 g) light brown sugar

1 tsp paprika

1 tsp ground cumin

12 asparagus spears, ends trimmed

1 cup (100 g) green beans

1 cup (210 g) dried orzo pasta

3 cups (720 ml) hot vegetable or chicken stock

2 cups (60 g) packed baby spinach leaves

8 grape tomatoes, quartered

Zest and juice of 1 lemon

⅓ cup (20 g) chopped fresh parsley

ROASTED VEGETABLE AND HERBY WILD RICE SALAD

This is a comforting warm salad with roasted veggies and rice. I like to sprinkle with shredded Parmesan before serving, but you can replace with a vegetarian hard cheese, if you prefer.

If you're not a vegetarian, this salad also tastes great with some crispy pancetta.

SERVES 4

Preheat the oven to 400°F (204°C).

On a large baking sheet, combine the chunks of sweet potato, red and yellow bell peppers and carrots.

In a small bowl, stir together the olive oil, garlic salt, salt, pepper, paprika and oregano and drizzle over the vegetables. Toss it all together, using your hands, then roast in the oven for 20 minutes, turning everything over after 10 minutes.

Add the red onion wedges and beet and toss everything together again so the onion and beet get coated with oil. Put back into the oven for an additional 10 to 12 minutes, or until the vegetables are tender and slightly charred at the edges.

Remove from the oven and transfer the roasted vegetables, plus any oil left on the pan, to a large serving bowl. Add the cooked wild rice, pea shoots and mixed herbs to the bowl.

Toss everything together and serve topped with the grated Parmesan and lemon wedges.

I large sweet potato, peeled and chopped into bite-size chunks

I red bell pepper, seeded and chopped into bite-size chunks

I yellow bell pepper, seeded and chopped into bite-size chunks

2 medium carrots, peeled and chopped into bite-size chunks

3 tbsp (45 ml) olive oil

½ tsp garlic salt

½ tsp salt

½ tsp freshly ground black pepper

I tsp smoked paprika

I tsp dried oregano

I red onion, chopped into wedges

I large beet, peeled and chopped into wedges

2 cups (333 g) cooked basmati and wild rice blend (about ⅔ cup [130 g] raw)

2 cups (40 g) packed pea shoots

I cup (60 g) packed mixed fresh herbs, such as cilantro, parsley and chives

2 tbsp (10 g) shredded Parmesan cheese

2 lemons, sliced into wedges

GARLIC CROUTON SALAD WITH BASIL AND MOZZARELLA

Way better than serving garlic bread, this Caprese-style salad with homemade garlic croutons always goes down a storm. I like to serve it as an appetizer for an Italian-themed meal, or as a side to accompany a simple pasta dish.

SERVES 4 AS AN APPETIZER OR SIDE DISH

Preheat the oven to 400°F (204°C). Place the ciabatta cubes on a baking sheet.

In a small bowl, mix together the melted butter, garlic, salt and parsley and brush all over the ciabatta cubes. Toast in the oven for 5 to 6 minutes, or until browned, then remove from the oven.

On a serving plate, arrange the garlic croutons with the tomatoes, mozzarella and basil.

In a small bowl, stir together the dressing ingredients. Drizzle on top of the salad before serving.

1 ciabatta bread, chopped into 1" (2.5-cm) cubes

¼ cup (60 ml) melted unsalted butter

3 cloves garlic, peeled and minced

½ tsp salt

3 tbsp (12 g) finely chopped fresh parsley

10 vine-ripened tomatoes, chopped into bite-size chunks

1 (4.5-oz [128-g]) ball buffalo mozzarella cheese, roughly torn

Small bunch of basil

BALSAMIC DRESSING

2 tbsp (30 ml) good-quality balsamic vinegar

1½ tbsp (23 ml) olive oil

Pinch of salt

Pinch of freshly ground black pepper

PANZANELLA SALAD WITH GOAT CHEESE CROUTONS

A fresh and flavorful Tuscan-style panzanella salad of crispy toasted ciabatta, softened in seasoned tomato juices. I like to give this salad a twist by topping it with panko-coated goat cheese croutons. The cheese melts a little and starts to ooze invitingly when it's lightly fried. So good!

I love that panzanella, which was originally thought of as peasant food—made to use up stale bread—now feels like a luxury meal. From humble beginnings to salad-y greatness!

SERVES 4

In a bowl, mix the tomatoes with the salt and pepper and set aside for 10 to 15 minutes, to release their juices.

In a skillet, heat the olive oil over medium-high heat, add the ciabatta chunks along with a pinch each of salt and pepper. Toast in the pan, turning often, until golden brown. This should take about 3 to 4 minutes.

Prepare the dressing. In a small pitcher, stir together all the dressing ingredients.

Once toasted, remove the ciabatta chunks from the skillet and add to the tomatoes. Add the cucumber and red onion and toss together to coat with the tomato juices.

Add half of the dressing and toss again. Set aside to marinate together while you make the goat cheese croutons.

To prepare the croutons, in a skillet, heat the oil over medium-high heat.

Take 2 plates and 1 shallow bowl. Stir together the flour and paprika on 1 plate. Crack the egg into the bowl and gently whisk for a few seconds with a fork. Stir together the bread crumbs and black pepper on the other plate. Dip each piece of goat cheese in turn into the flour, egg and finally the bread crumbs, shaking off any excess as you go.

Fry the croutons in the skillet, turning every minute or two, for 5 to 6 minutes, or until golden and crisp on all sides.

Divide the tomato and ciabatta salad among 4 serving plates and top with the goat cheese croutons and basil leaves. Serve with the remaining dressing.

10 vine-ripened tomatoes, chopped

¼ tsp salt, plus a pinch more

¼ tsp freshly ground black pepper, plus a pinch more

2 tbsp (30 ml) olive oil

1 ciabatta bread, chopped into bite-size chunks

1 cucumber, peeled, seeded and sliced into half-moons

1 red onion, thinly sliced

Small bunch of basil

RED WINE DRESSING

¼ cup (60 ml) olive oil

2 tbsp (30 ml) red wine vinegar

1 tsp superfine sugar

1 clove garlic, peeled and minced

Pinch of salt

Pinch of freshly ground black pepper

GOAT CHEESE CROUTONS

2 tbsp (30 ml) olive oil

3 tbsp (25 g) all-purpose flour

¼ tsp paprika

1 large egg

Heaping 6 tbsp (45 g) panko bread crumbs

¼ tsp freshly ground black pepper

7 oz (198 g) firm goat cheese, chopped into bite-size chunks

CREAMY POTATO SALAD

A creamy, tangy potato salad that goes down a storm at any barbecue or picnic. Being based in the United Kingdom, I use a condiment called salad cream in this salad for my dad's traditional version. It's difficult to find salad cream anywhere else, so after much testing, I've made this version—which tastes even better!

SERVES 4

Place the potatoes in a pan and cover with cold water. Bring to a boil and simmer for 8 to 9 minutes, or until tender. Drain the potatoes and set aside to cool.

In a bowl, mash the anchovies to a paste with a fork. Add the onion, mayonnaise, Worcestershire sauce, mustard, vinegar, salt and white pepper and mix together.

Carefully fold in the potatoes until coated with the sauce. Taste and add a little more seasoning, if needed.

Cover and refrigerate for at least 30 minutes or up to a day before serving. Just before serving, sprinkle with the chopped chives.

5 medium potatoes, peeled and chopped into bite-size chunks

2 anchovies

½ small yellow onion, chopped very finely

6 tbsp (84 g) mayonnaise

1 tsp Worcestershire sauce

1 tsp Dijon mustard

1 tsp white wine vinegar

¼ tsp salt

Good pinch of ground white pepper

1 tbsp (3 g) finely chopped fresh chives

GARLIC AND HERB NEW POTATO SALAD

A delicious warm potato salted with garlic butter and fresh peas—perfect for a simple spring lunch. This also makes a great side dish for barbecues and garden parties!

SERVES 4

Place the potatoes in a pan and cover with cold water. Bring to a boil, then simmer for 15 minutes, or until tender, adding the peas to the water for the final 3 minutes. Drain in a colander and set aside.

Give the pan you cooked the potatoes in a quick dry and add the butter, olive oil, garlic, salt and pepper. Heat over medium heat until the butter melts and the garlic releases its fragrance, about 1 minute. Turn off the heat.

Add the potatoes and peas back to the pan, along with the chives and scallions and all but a tablespoon (4 g) of the parsley. Carefully toss together to coat in the garlic butter.

On a serving plate, arrange the mâche and top with the potato mixture. Place the radish slices on top and sprinkle on the crumbled feta. Finish with the remaining parsley and a pinch of pepper before serving.

1 lb (454 g) baby new potatoes, sliced in half

1 cup (150 g) freshly shelled peas

2 tbsp (28 g) unsalted butter

2 tbsp (30 ml) olive oil

2 cloves garlic, peeled and minced

½ tsp salt

½ tsp freshly ground black pepper, plus a pinch for serving

2 tbsp (6 g) finely chopped fresh chives

6 scallions, sliced

⅓ cup (20 g) chopped fresh parsley, divided

2 cups (40 g) packed mâche

3 radishes, thinly sliced

½ cup (75 g) crumbled feta cheese

FRUIT-BASED SALAD SUPERSTARS

It would be remiss of me to stick to savory salads for the whole of this book, so I've included a few of my fruity favorites.

You might notice I include fruits in many of my savory salads, too. Sliced figs, apples and pears make a great addition to any salad to lift the flavors and make them more interesting. A sprinkling of pomegranate seeds or some chopped dried apricots work wonders, too.

A fruit salad doesn't have to start and end with a bowl of chopped-up fruit.

Sometimes a fruit salad deserves a dressing, too! Apple caramel sauce, almond-flavored honey or a simple spoonful of Greek yogurt turns a salad into dessert (or an awesome breakfast!).

The first salad in this section is a mixture of sweet and savory—wedges of watermelon with homemade tapenade and feta. The rest of the salads are most definitely on the sweeter side.

WATERMELON SALAD WITH MICRO SHOOTS AND TAPENADE DRESSING

The salty richness of this tapenade works so well with the juicy sweetness of the watermelon. I like to serve it with micro shoots and feta for a salad that packs a punch. You can also serve it as a party food if you pile the micro shoots, feta and tapenade on top of wedges of watermelon.

SERVES 4

Slice the watermelon into ½-inch (1.3-cm) slices. Slice each piece into 1-inch (2.5-cm) triangles.

Arrange three-quarters of the micro shoots on a plate and layer the watermelon slices on top.

Sprinkle the rest of the micro shoots on top, along with the crumbled feta.

In a food processor combine all the dressing ingredients and pulse a few times, until just combined.

Place little drops of the dressing on top of the watermelon salad and sprinkle with a pinch of salt and black pepper before serving.

1 (5-lb [2.25-kg]) watermelon

2 cups (50 g) micro shoots

¼ cup (38 g) crumbled feta

Pinch of salt

Pinch of freshly ground black pepper

TAPENADE DRESSING

1 cup (155 g) black olives, pitted

2 tbsp (17 g) capers

4 anchovy fillets

1 clove garlic, peeled and minced

Juice of 1 lemon

⅓ cup (20 g) finely chopped fresh parsley

3 tbsp (45 ml) extra virgin olive oil

Pinch of salt

Pinch of freshly ground black pepper

COCONUT BROWN RICE BERRY SALAD WITH MANGO AND MINT

A great brunch or dessert—this sweet rice salad is a bit of a twist on rice pudding. The coconut milk adds a lovely sweetness. I cook the rice so it's tender but you can still see the individual rice grains. If you want a creamier rice-pudding style, you can stir in an extra cup (240 ml) of coconut milk and a splash of heavy cream and let it cook for a few minutes longer.

SERVES 4

In a saucepan, combine the rice with the vanilla and coconut milk. Stir together, bring to a boil, cover and lower the heat to very low.

Cook for 45 to 50 minutes, checking a few times during the last 15 minutes—top up with a little more coconut milk, if necessary, but it's likely it won't have all absorbed—or until the rice is tender. You want it to have a little bit of bite rather than be too soggy like rice pudding.

Drain and allow to cool to room temperature, then sprinkle with 3 tablespoons (16 g) of the toasted coconut and fluff the rice with a fork.

In a serving bowl, combine the rice with the blueberries, blackberries, strawberries and mango, and gently mix.

Top with the remaining tablespoon (5 g) of coconut, plus the pistachios and mint.

Serve with a drizzle of honey.

1 cup (198 g) uncooked brown rice

½ tsp vanilla extract

3 cups (720 ml) coconut milk beverage (from a carton, not a can)

¼ cup (21 g) unsweetened shredded coconut, toasted, divided

1 cup (145 g) blueberries

1 cup (145 g) blackberries

1 cup (167 g) hulled and chopped strawberries

1 mango, peeled, pitted and chopped into bite-size chunks

¼ cup (30 g) pistachios, roughly chopped

Small bunch of fresh mint, for garnish

Honey or golden syrup, for serving

PINEAPPLE, PEACH AND BERRY SALAD WITH APPLE CARAMEL SAUCE

Just a heads up: This makes a *lot* of apple caramel sauce—around 2 cups (480 ml). Personally, I like a lot of caramel sauce, so we're good. If you have any leftover sauce, you can cover and refrigerate it for up to a week. Perfect for drizzling on muffins, in oatmeal or just dipping in your finger for a sneaky taste whenever you open the refrigerator.

I love it drizzled over juicy fresh fruit for a tasty dessert.

SERVES 4

For the sauce, peel, core and chop the apples into ½-inch (1.3-cm) cubes. Place in a saucepan with ¼ cup (50 g) of the sugar. Heat over medium heat, stirring every minute or so, until the apples break down and the sugar dissolves, about 15 minutes. Turn off the heat, let cool for a few minutes and then carefully blend the apples to a smooth puree, using an immersion blender. Alternatively, cool completely and process in a food processor.

Pour the remaining ¼ cup (50 g) of sugar into a clean saucepan and smooth out into an even layer. Heat over medium-low heat until the edges of the sugar start to melt, then start to stir with a silicone spatula. Stir often, until all the sugar dissolves. It will be lumpy at first, but will eventually melt down.

Carefully add the butter, 1 chunk at a time (it will spit, so take care). Once all of the butter has been added, stir together.

The sauce will separate, but that's fine. Add the cream very slowly, while stirring (it will start to froth), then simmer, stirring occasionally, for an additional minute. Turn off the heat.

Add the apple puree to the caramel and stir together until incorporated.

Assemble the salad. On a serving plate, arrange the pineapple, peaches, strawberries and raspberries and drizzle with a little of the sauce.

Top with the toasted hazelnuts and a few mint leaves and serve with the remaining sauce.

TIP: You can buy ready-toasted hazelnuts or toast them yourself in a dry skillet over medium heat, stirring often to toast them evenly, for 2 to 3 minutes, or until lightly golden.

APPLE CARAMEL SAUCE

2 large Bramley apples

½ cup (200 g) sugar, divided

5½ tbsp (80 g) unsalted butter, cut into small chunks

½ cup (120 ml) heavy cream

SALAD

1 small pineapple, peeled and chopped into bite-size chunks

2 peaches, pitted and chopped

1 cup (167 g) strawberries, hulled and quartered

1 cup (120 g) raspberries

1 tbsp (7 g) chopped, toasted hazelnuts (see Tip)

Small bunch fresh mint leaves, for garnish

ORANGE SALAD WITH PISTACHIOS AND POMEGRANATE

A light and delicate dessert salad that looks impressive on the dinner table, yet only takes a few minutes to put together. I've added some Ruby Red grapefruit and clementines to the oranges for a splash of color, but you can just stick to oranges if you prefer. Blood oranges make an amazing addition when they're in season.

SERVES 4

Using a sharp knife remove the skin from the grapefruit, clementines and oranges. Slice the fruits into thin slices and arrange on a serving plate.

In a small bowl, stir together the honey and almond extract and drizzle over the fruit.

Scatter the pistachios, mint and thyme leaves on top, then finish with a sprinkling of pomegranate arils and rose petals.

1 Ruby Red grapefruit

2 clementines

2 oranges

2 tbsp (40 g) honey

½ tsp French almond extract

¼ cup (30 g) pistachios, roughly chopped

Small bunch of fresh mint, for garnish

Small bunch of fresh thyme, for garnish

Arils of 1 pomegranate (see Tips on page 125)

1 tbsp (0.3 g) culinary-grade dried rose petals

GRILLED FRUIT SALAD WITH BROWN SUGAR AND GREEK YOGURT

Grilling sugar-dusted fruit really brings out those gorgeous flavors.

I like to add fresh strawberries and lime zest to the serving dish for a splash of color, plus a good dollop of creamy Greek yogurt with honey for dipping.

This is a yummy dessert for summer!

SERVES 4

Heat a dry grill pan or large skillet over high heat.

Meanwhile, place the prepared mango, pineapple, peaches and plums on a cutting board and sprinkle with the brown sugar and cinnamon. Move the fruit about in the sugar to coat.

Place the fruit on the hot pan, ensuring the peaches and plums are sliced side down, and cook until grill lines appear, for 2 to 4 minutes.

Remove the peaches and plums as they'll go too soft if left on the pan for too long.

Turn over the mango and pineapple to cook the other side for another minute or two. Then, remove from the pan.

On a serving plate, arrange the grilled fruits, place the strawberries on top and spoon the Greek yogurt over it all.

Drizzle with honey and sprinkle with the lime zest and mint leaves before serving.

1 mango, peeled, pitted and sliced

1 small pineapple, peeled, cored and chopped into bite-size chunks

2 peaches, pitted and sliced

2 plums, pitted and sliced

¼ cup (60 g) light brown muscovado sugar

½ tsp ground cinnamon

10 strawberries, hulled and sliced in half

1 cup (240 g) Greek yogurt

1 tbsp (20 g) honey

Zest of 1 lime

Small bunch of fresh mint, for garnish

BONUS SALAD DRESSINGS

SWEET CHILE MANGO DRESSING
(PAGE 182)

EASY TZATZIKI DRESSING
(PAGE 182)

3-HERB AND GARLIC DRESSING
(PAGE 183)

It's great to have a selection of simple salad dressings up your sleeve to bring the flavors together for a complex salad, or to make a simple bowl of leaves more interesting.

Salad dressings can really help to define a salad by complementing or enhancing flavors, adding sweetness, tanginess or even a bit of spicy chili heat.

I've included dressings with a lot of my recipes that you can use as they are, or swap around to go with different salads. I've also included six additional dressing recipes here—because you can never have too many!

CREAMY CHIMICHURRI DRESSING
(PAGE 183)

HONEY SESAME GINGER MISO DRESSING
(PAGE 184)

SMOKY CAJUN BUTTERMILK DRESSING
(PAGE 184)

SWEET CHILE MANGO DRESSING

This tangy, sweet dressing works well with chicken or tuna steak salads. One-quarter teaspoon of red pepper flakes is enough for a hint of heat, but if you like it hotter (as I do), go for ½ teaspoon.

In a small blender or mini food processor, combine all the ingredients, except the cilantro. Pulse until smooth, then stir in the cilantro.

1 ripe mango, peeled, pitted and roughly chopped

1 tbsp (15 ml) white wine vinegar

2 tbsp (30 ml) olive oil

2 tbsp (30 ml) water

1 clove garlic, peeled

¼ tsp red pepper flakes

¼ tsp salt

¼ tsp freshly ground black pepper

2 tbsp (5 g) finely chopped fresh cilantro

EASY TZATZIKI DRESSING

I make this dressing for every barbecue! It goes so well with barbecued meats, as well as lamb and falafel all served up with a big Greek salad.

Slice the cucumber in half lengthwise and scoop out the seeds with a teaspoon.

Grate the cucumber, then, over the sink or a bowl, squeeze the shredded cucumber in your hands to remove any excess liquid.

Place the cucumber in a bowl along with the remaining ingredients and stir together until combined.

½ large cucumber

7 oz (200 g) Greek yogurt (full-fat works best)

1 tsp white wine vinegar

½ tsp dried dill, or 1 tbsp (4 g) fresh, chopped

½ small clove garlic, peeled and crushed

½ tsp sugar

¼ tsp salt

3-HERB AND GARLIC DRESSING

This is a fresh and flavorful herb-packed dressing that works well with steak and duck salads.

In a small bowl, stir together all the ingredients until combined.

⅓ cup (80 ml) olive oil

2 tbsp (30 ml) red wine vinegar

¼ tsp salt

¼ tsp freshly ground black pepper

½ clove garlic, peeled and minced

1 tbsp (20 g) honey

3 tbsp (8 g) finely chopped fresh cilantro

3 tbsp (12 g) finely chopped fresh parsley

3 tbsp (9 g) finely chopped chives

CREAMY CHIMICHURRI DRESSING

This is a lightly spiced chimichurri with a creamy twist. This dressing works with most leafy salads, especially with red meat.

In a small bowl, stir together all the ingredients until combined.

½ cup (30 g) packed fresh parsley, chopped

½ cup (20 g) packed fresh cilantro, chopped

¼ tsp red pepper flakes

¼ cup (60 ml) olive oil

2 cloves garlic, peeled and minced

¼ tsp salt

¼ tsp freshly ground black pepper

¼ tsp dried oregano

1 tbsp (15 ml) fresh lemon juice

1 tsp white wine vinegar

⅓ cup (75 g) mayonnaise

⅓ cup (77 g) sour cream

HONEY SESAME GINGER MISO DRESSING

Full of umami flavor, this Asian-style dressing works well with salmon, chicken, noodles and julienned vegetables.

In a small bowl, stir together all the ingredients until combined.

2 tbsp (32 g) white miso paste

1 tbsp (15 ml) olive oil

1 tbsp (15 ml) sesame oil

1 tbsp (15 ml) rice vinegar

1 tbsp (15 ml) fresh lemon juice

2 tbsp (40 g) honey

1 clove garlic, peeled and minced

1 tsp minced fresh ginger

¼ tsp freshly ground black pepper

½ tsp red pepper flakes

½ tsp sesame seeds

SMOKY CAJUN BUTTERMILK DRESSING

I love this creamy Cajun dressing with chicken and shrimp (especially if they're crispy coated!). The slight spiciness works really well with snap peas and other sweet, crunchy vegetables.

In a small bowl, stir together all the ingredients until combined.

½ cup (20 g) mayonnaise

½ cup (120 ml) buttermilk

1 clove garlic, peeled and minced

1 tsp fresh lemon juice

½ tsp smoked paprika

1 tsp Cajun seasoning

¼ tsp onion powder

1 tbsp (4 g) fresh dill, chopped

1 tbsp (3 g) fresh chives, chopped

Pinch of salt

Pinch of freshly ground black pepper

ACKNOWLEDGMENTS

I would like to thank my husband Chris for his never-ending support, both during the writing of this book and throughout my journey from the corporate IT world to the world of cooking, photography and writing. I'm thrilled that he's since joined me as my business partner and we get to work with each other every day.

I'd also like to thank our children Gracey and Lewis for their super-helpful attitudes and being my chief recipe testers.

Thank you to my mum and dad for starting me off with my love of food and cooking at an early age and building my confidence in the kitchen.

Thanks also to my mother-in-law Kath for always jumping in whenever things get crazy and I need help!

Thank you to my blog readers for continuing to come back to read, cook and comment on my recipes—I LOVE reading every single one of them.

And finally, I'd like to thank everyone at Page Street Publishing, including my editor Marissa Giambelluca for her ideas and support, and creative director Meg Baskis and team for their advice and design of my book.

ABOUT THE AUTHOR

Nicky Corbishley is an award-winning food blogger who lives in the UK with her husband Chris and their two children, Gracey and Lewis.

After a 14-year career in corporate IT, Nicky wanted to do something more creative, whilst being able to spend more time with her children. With a life-long passion for cooking (and eating!), her blog Kitchen Sanctuary was born.

Initially it was intended to be a diary of her recipes, but it quickly grew, and Nicky was able to turn it into a full-time career towards the end of 2015. Chris joined her in 2017 and they now spend their days doing what they love—creating recipes and doing food photography and videography both for the blog and as freelancers.

Visit her at kitchensanctuary.com for delicious family-friendly recipes and livingtheblog.com for blogging tips and tricks.

INDEX